Tamm's Textbook

AP* U.S. History student workbook containing vocabulary and chapter assignments to use with:

Henretta, Hinderaker, Edwards & Self's

America's History⁺

8th edition (Country music painting cover)

Coursepak Series A   **Independently Made**

David Tamm

For the 3%

---

*Advanced Placement program and AP are registered trademarks of the College Board, which was not involved in the production of, and does not endorse, this product.

⁺America's History 8th edition is written by James A. Henretta, Eric Hinderaker, Rebecca Edwards and Robert O. Self, and published by Bedford St. Martin's. These parties were not involved in the production of, and do not endorse, this product.

Cover Image: A man looks in a bucket at something very like the Thomas Hart Benton painting.

Copyright © 2016

CONTENTS

This resource book is organized in the following way to integrate with *America's History, 8th edition:*

Suggested Year and Weekly Plan

Vocab and Chapter Assignments

Addenda: Crash Course, Test Correction Forms, Movie Review Forms & More

LICENSING

Teachers are fully licensed by the copyright holder to copy individual worksheets out of this book in whatever quantity is needed for classroom use. Students may also order a full workbook as a consumable to write in throughout the year. These materials may not be distributed online in any form or shared with other teachers without expressed written permission.

When given as a full workbook, this material improves content coherency, student enjoyment, parent appreciation, and teacher satisfaction."

-State of Florida Certified Teacher

"Sublimely usable."

"Great as weekly assignments"

"Spend one hour's pay, save 300 hours' planning time!"

"Rocket into the frontier of utility!"

"Textbooks are expensive. With this workbook, you get your money's worth!"

"They read the book, which is the main issue many have."

"Perfect if there's a substitute"

"Very progressive."

Suggested Year Plan

A good thing about *America's History* is its number of chapters. Most schools begin in late August or early September, leaving ~30 weeks to get through the book if you want any time for review before the exam. Some books, however, have 38-41 chapters, making it hard to do 'a chapter a week' and still have time for review at the end. With 31 chapters, the Henretta text is good on this, especially if you want to enjoy the semblance of military-style structure. What follows is the book contents, and a blast from the past of how this course was ordered when it was young.

America's History 8th edition
Henretta, Hinderaker, Edwards & Self, 2014
Weekly Breakdown

A History of Our Country
David S. Muzzey, 1942
Flashback

Week 1: Ch. 1	Colliding Worlds	Europe Wakes and Stretches
Week 2: Ch. 2	American Experiments	A Century of Exploration
Week 3: Ch. 3	The British-Atlantic World	The English Settlements
Week 4: Ch. 4	Growth, Diversity and Conflict	Colonial America
Week 5: Ch. 5	The Problem of Empire	Liberty or Loyalty?
Week 6: Ch. 6	Making War & Republican Gov'ts	Washington Sees it Through
Week 7: Ch. 7	Hammering out a Federal Republic	Confederation and Constitution
Week 8: Ch. 8	Creating a Republican Culture	Launching the Government
Week 9: Ch. 9	Transforming the Economy	Jefferson makes a Great Bargain
Week 10: Ch. 10	A Democratic Revolution	Our Second War for Independence
Week 11: Ch. 11	Religion and Reform	Sectional Rivalry
Week 12: Ch. 12	The South: Slavery and Society	The Jacksonian Era
Week 13: Ch. 13	Expansion, War & Sectional Crisis	Advance to the Pacific
Week 14: Ch. 14	Two Societies at War	The Businessman's Peace
Week 15: Ch. 15	Reconstruction	The House Divided
Week 16: Ch. 16	Conquering a Continent	The Civil War
Week 17: Ch. 17	Industrial America: Corp. & Conflict	Reconstruction
Week 18: Ch. 18	The Victorians Make the Modern	The New Industrial Age
Week 19: Ch. 19	"Civilization's Inferno"	Futile Party Battles
Week 20: Ch. 20	Whose Government?	The Rising of the West
Week 21: Ch. 21	An Emerging World Power	Dominion Over Palm and Pine
Week 22: Ch. 22	Cultural Conflict: Bubble & Bust	The Roosevelt Era
Week 23: Ch. 23	Managing the Great Depression	The Progressive Movement
Week 24: Ch. 24	The World at War	Wilson and the 'New Freedom'
Week 25: Ch. 25	Cold War America	The Struggle for Neutrality
Week 26: Ch. 26	Triumph of the Middle Class	Our Part in the Fighting
Week 27: Ch. 27	Walking into Freedom Land	Influence of the War on Life
Week 28: Ch. 28	Uncivil Wars	Our Part in the Peace
Week 29: Ch. 29	Search for Order in an Era of Limits	The Aftermath of the War
Week 30: Ch. 30	Conservative America in Ascent	The Program of 'Normalcy'
Week 31: Ch. 31	Confronting Dilemmas	Worshipping the Golden Calf
		The Eclipse of Prosperity
		The 'Hundred Days'
		The New Deal on Trial
		Entering a New Decade

Suggested Weekly Plan

Manic Moon Day
It is recommended that students have a lecture overview of the key points in each chapter, take notes, and discuss the concepts involved. Even though teachers are discouraged in parts of the country from lecturing, the speed of the AP* U.S. History course necessitates some direct teacher-student transmission of content. The chapter assignment forms presented herein could be used as a guide during the discussion.

Textbook Tiw's Day
Most school districts encourage pair or group work. This can be used to positive effect if students mine the textbook (or a review book) in class and either jigsaw the chapter, presenting their take on part of the whole, or jointly venture to find the answers to the specific problems in history. The activities herein lend themselves to this kind of classroom setting too. Groups can, for example, take part of each chapter assignment and focus on that, and then discuss their part whole group.

Writing Woden's Day
The AP* U.S. History curriculum is reading and writing intensive, and brainstorming (diagramming) solutions to mini-FRQs is a good way to build up key thinking processes helpful in expressing oneself in writing. Another helpful way is practicing good old-fashioned reading comprehension, but as many teachers know, the content of the passages is key to student growth and success. The material has to be interesting, and luckily, U.S. History has a great potential interest value. If you find the current materials helpful and of high enough quality, you may want to obtain the companion volume to this book, *Tamm's Textbook Tools Coursepak Series B: Reading Shorts, Writings and Online Activities*, on *Amazon.com* or another platform.

Technetronic Thor's Day
Many AP* teachers try to bring in technology to the classroom, whether in the form of a laptop cart, or by taking students to a media lab. Increasingly, students are using their own mobile devices. *Kahoot.it* is now popular as a Jeopardy-style review game, joining *Quizlet* and a vast number of other review materials available online. A good directory to websites usable with AP U.S. History classes, including the Bailey textbook site with history activities, is located at Antarcticaedu.com/US.htm. Included in the addendum to this volume is a Crash Course viewer response sheet that can be given as homework on Thursday nights, or completed as an in-class review assignment.

Fantastic Frija's Day
It is suggested that students take a 25-50-question test once a week. That means a couple chapters might have to be doubled up. A timed, 35 min. period should be reserved in class- or in some cases out depending on how nice you are- to do a weekly 50 question test. If this happens on Friday, it is recommended students take home the chapter assignments for the next week's chapter, or at least part of it, for homework. Doing just the vocab, for example, is itself is a good way to introduce a new chapter.

Now let's get down to business!

Manic Monday

and

Textbook Tuesday

Chapter Activities

Pg. 6   **1 – COLLIDING WORLDS**   **Explorer**_____

Nothing like a first impression

What surprised you most about the passages:

Columbus in Spain	*De Soto and the Lady of Cofachiqui*	*Lopez in Kongo*

Pic 7: Look closely and note four different things going on in this picture of the Algonquian village:

1)   2)

3)   4)

Mesoamerica _____

Bering Strait _____

"Eskimos" _____

What is the estimated population of the following regions upon the arrival of Europeans?

Central Mexico: *Andes Region:*

List three important Mesoamerican crops:

Tribute _____

Aztec Empire _____

Tenochtitlan _____

List six important trade goods:	Describe the importance of human sacrifice in Aztec culture:

Map 9: What is the general timeframe for the existence of the land bridge?	What was the environment of *your* state like in this era?

Map 10: List the tribes by modern-day country and lifestyle:

	Canada	United States	Mexico/Caribbean
Agriculture			
Hunting-Gathering			
Fishing-Gathering			

Cahokia

Pic 11: Do a quick sketch of Tenochtitlan. Make sure to include the "Temple Sacrificant" and the famous causeways: _____

"To the Aztecs, Tenochtitlan was more than the capital of their empire." Do you agree or disagree with this statement? Why?

Mississippians

Pic 12: The Great Serpent Mound, made around _____, is in the State of _____.

Describe the Powhatan Chiefdom's political structure at the time of the American founding:

Iroquois Confederacy _____

Hiawatha _____

America Compared 14. Answer the Questions for Analysis below:

1)

2)

_____

Matriarchal _____

Five Nations _____

Describe the situation in the following places:

The Great Lakes   *The Great Plains and Rockies*

The Arid Southwest   *The Pacific Coast*

_____

Pic 16: This spoon was found in: | Pic 17: This bowl was found in:

a. the Great Lakes area   b. the Southwest | a. the Pacific Northwest   b. the Great Plains

Animists _____

Blood feud _____

Hierarchy _____

Patriarchy _____

Primogeniture _____

Peasants _____

Republic

Pic 19: Sketch the graph and label the reasons for the cycle's "high" points:

```
       |           |           |           |           |
 120   |           |           |           |           |
       |           |           |           |           |
 100   |-----------|-----------|-----------|-----------|
       |           |           |           |           |
  80   |           |           |           |           |
       |           |           |           |           |
```

The Basilica of San Marco in Venice is best described as: a. plain   b. ornate

Civic humanism

Renaissance

How did the growth of commerce shift the structure of power in European societies?

Guilds

Christianity

The Roman emperor who legalized Christianity was _____.

The official language of the Catholic Church continued to be _____ even after the fall of Rome.

Pic 21: Based on what Michael the Archangel is doing here, it is fair to say that the Christian conception of morality was:

a. Relative (depended on the person's opinion)   *b. Absolute (right and wrong are not negotiable)*

Heresies

Islam

Crusades

How did the following influence the Protestant Reformation:

    Martin Luther   *John Calvin*

Counter-Reformation

Some of the traditions of Sudanic Africa include: | Some of the more important kingdoms of West Africa included:

Trans-Sahara trade

Map 24: List tribal-ethnic groups located in the following areas:

<u>Senegal-Gambia Rivers</u>   <u>Grain, Ivory, Gold and Slave coasts</u>   <u>Niger River</u>   <u>Congo River</u>

Pic 25: Aside from being a riding animal and beast of burden, what else was a horse in Malian society? | Aside from many wives and children, what else made a man happy in Mali?

Caravel

Lateen sail

Thinking Like a Historian 26. Answer the 'Analyzing the Evidence' section:

1)

2)

3)

Pic 28: Describe the geographical setting of the Kongo capital of Banza:

_____

Map 29: Name the voyagers who accomplished the following:

A trip from Portugal to South Africa's Cape of Good Hope _____

A trip from Portugal to India around Africa _____

A trip from Spain to the Caribbean _____

A trip from Britain to Canada _____

A trip from Spain to the Caribbean and into the American South _____

Six reasons Africans held other Africans in slavery were:

1)   2)   3)

4)   5)   6)

About how many Africans were transported to the Middle East as slaves along the Trans-Saharan route?	Map 30: Why might Ferdinand and Isabella have been more persuaded by this map to sponsor Columbus than if it had been accurate?
_____	
For over 700 years, Spanish Christians and Arab and Moorish Muslims had fought in Spain. The term for the Christian victory there is:	

1492

Map 31: The city Columbus founded on Hispaniola was and is still called:	During the conquest of the Aztecs, Cortes' ships landed near the present-day Mexican city of:

American Voices 32. Answer the Questions for Analysis below:

1)

2)

3)

Nuevo Mundo

Las Indias

Pic 34: Was the Mexica (Aztec) counterattack shown here ultimately successful?	What was the 'silent ally' of the Spanish & why?

Note the significance of the following explorers:

Amerigo Vespucci	Ponce De Leon	Vasco de Balboa	Pedro Cabral

Map 36: Sketch out a freehand (or trace) this lavish map of early Brazil and draw in some of the things the cartographers working for King Manuel I found noteworthy:

Timeline 39. Put the following in correct chronological order:

Anasazi, Aztecs, Cabral, Cahokia, Cortes, Iroquois, Mississippians, Pizarro

Pg. 40 **2 – AMERICAN EXPERIMENTS** **Colonist** _____

If we name our first colony on Mars after Captain Kirk, will it be called Jamestown too?

Chattel slavery

What was the purpose of the 1662 Virginia statute?

Describe the characteristics of the three types of colonies that emerged in the New World:

Tribute colonies	*Plantation colonies*	*Neo-Europes*

Pic 41: Lord Baltimore is holding a map of Maryland, why? | Whose outfit do you like the best of the three?

Encomiendas

Potosi

What is inflation, and why did Spain's silver mining cause it at the turn of the 17th century?

Mestizo

Zambo

'Casta system'

Timeline 42: Highlight the timeline with the correct dates and labels:

Columbian Exchange

Note some things that spread from the Old World to the New World: | Note things that spread from the New World to the Old World:

Pic 43: How did the disease shown here influence dramatically the course of history in the New World?

_____

Henry VIII _____

Elizabeth I _____

Pic 45: Name the religious divide that caused Elizabeth I and Philip II of Spain to be adversarial:	Name the political-economic divide that caused the two to be adversarial:

Map 46: Note the names of the plantation colonies in the following areas:

    British America   *Spanish America*   *Portuguese America*

_____

Sugarcane _____

Tobacco _____

Jamestown _____

Pic 47: An Indian word that made its way into the English language is:	Map 48: What happened to the Roanoke colony shown on this map by John White?

Map 48 (r.): Name the body (bodies) of water associated with the following settlements

_____ Montreal, Quebec   _____ Plymouth, Salem, Providence

_____ New Amsterdam (New York)   _____ Jamestown

Pic 49: How was John Smith's life spared, according to the accounts? _____

Powhatan _____

John Smith _____

Pocahontas _____

John Rolfe _____

The cash crop that 'saved' the Jamestown colony was _____

Thinking Like a Historian 26. Answer the 'Analyzing the Evidence' section:

1)

2)

3)

4)

House of Burgesses

| How did King James, of Jamestown fame, respond to the 1622 Indian uprising? | Why did King Charles allow Lord Baltimore to establish the Maryland colony? |

Act of Toleration

Which cash crops did the Caribbean islands start producing? _____

Pic 53: The crop being harvested and processed here can be considered:

a. one of the easier cash crops to grow   *b. one of the most difficult cash crops to grow*

Freehold

Headright system

Indentured servitude

Map 54. There are four questions being asked by the white boxes on this map. Answer them:

NW)

SW)

NE)

SE)

Graph 55: What demographic change caused the percentage of whites in the labor force to go down?	What did the first African slaves to the future United States labor on?

Note the accomplishments of the following French explorers:

Jacques Cartier

Samuel de Champlain

Robert de La Salle

Why was the large French-controlled area in the middle of the U.S. named 'Louisiana'?

Henry Hudson

New Netherland

As opposed to cash crops in the British, Spanish and Portuguese-controlled territories, the trade in this resource was the major moneymaker of French and Dutch America:	Pic 58: Why were the palisades so prominent a feature in 'old' New York?

Map 59: Note the trade goods originating in the following places:

Mexico and the Caribbean:

Europe and Russia:

Africa:

The Middle East:

India:

The East Indies:

China:

Iroquois

Beaver Wars

Pilgrims

Mayflower

William Bradford

Puritans

John Winthrop

Masachusetts Bay

What did Winthrop mean when he said "[We] should be as a City upon a Hill?"	Do you think Americans still have a responsibility to themselves or to the world to be a 'shining' example?

Map 61. Note the numbers of migrants from Britain to the following:

```
    \
     |
America |
    /

     o o o
Caribbean
     o o o
```

```
        /\
        | |_
        /__\

         Britain
        (just go with it)
```

Joint-stock corporation

Predestination

Roger Williams

Toleration

Anne Hutchinson

Note the difference between a 'covenant of works' and a 'covenant of grace':

Pic 63: The Almanac shown here can be best described as: a. anti-catholic   b. a farmer's handbook

Witchcraft

Salem Witch Trial

Yeoman

Town meeting

Pic 64: Why were the puritanical Puritans uneasy about the items worn in this picture?

Map 65: What was the main determinant as to why these settlements are so differently laid out?

Pic 66: For what purpose did the Huron Indians bury their dead above ground as shown here?

Pic 67: If you asked your parent about Metacom they'd likely be confused. That's because in their textbook when they were in high school, it was called King Philip's War. Why?

American Voices 68. Answer the Questions for Analysis below:

1)

2)

3)

Metacom's War

Bacon's Rebellion

William Berkeley

Pic 71: If you were a lawyer arguing both sides of the case of Nathanial Bacon in court, what arguments would you use to convince of jury of the following:

Nathanial Bacon is a 'rebel and traitor'　　　　　*Nathanial Bacon is a hero*

Pg. 80   3 – THE BRITISH ATLANTIC WORLD   Pilgrim_____

Better grab your Penn and get started Pilgrim, or you'll be Quakin', 'cause the Acts of Toleration don't cover sloth! Seriously. They don't.

Note the results of the Lancaster Conference of 1744 | Pic 81: Why was this image made and do you think it would be found there today?

_____

William Penn _____

Proprietorships _____

The Quakers were also known as: | The Quakers   *liked*   *disliked*   the manorial system.

_____ | Their example was   *Bradford*   *Bacon*

Describe the Quakers' overall philosophy:

_____

Chart 83: Which of the colonies established by 1750 did not become a future state? _____

Navigation Acts _____

Pic 84: The caption speculates this painting had a political purpose as well as an aesthetic one. What sorts of things in the painting do you think were included to fulfill that purpose?

_____

If you were a lawyer arguing both sides of the case, what arguments would you provide in favor of the following (use the chart on pg. 85 if you can figure out how it can bolster your arguments):

    Edward Randolph | *The Massachusetts Bay Assembly*

Dominion of N.E. _____

Edmund Andros _____

Map 87: What modern-day states made up part of the Dominion of New England?

_____

Glorious Revolution _____

John Locke _____

Declaration of Rights _____

Pic 86: What is a 'Leviathan' as shown here on the cover of Thomas Hobbes' 1651 book?

_____

If you were a lawyer arguing both sides of the case, what arguments would you use to support the following contentions:

Hobbes is right b/c order and authority are the true safeguards from anarchy- and are more important than 'rights'	*John Locke is right b/c people's individual and natural rights are most important, namely life, liberty and property*
Do you think Locke 'invented' what we know of as human rights, or do they come from some other, non-human source?	*Who do you agree with more?*

Constitutional monarchs _____

Second Hundred Years' War _____

Tribalization _____

Covenant chain _____

Chart 88: Note which of the wars saw an outcome that was positive for Great Britain:

_____

After reading the section entitled 'Indian Goals,' what do you think Native Americans had to gain by siding with one or another European or colonial power?

_____

South Atlantic System

Map 91: In which region did blacks outnumber whites by a great margin?	Why is the year 1713 so important for this map?
Chart 92. Copy as closely as you can this chart's bubbles and figures. They say you can't draw a perfect circle freehand- try to prove 'them' wrong!	According to the *Wealth of Nations*, what was the most profitable cash crop? _____ How often did a British ship leave Africa with slaves in the 1790s? _____ If the African 'King of Barsally' wanted goods or Brandy, how did he get them? _____ Map 93: Leaving Luanda, use the inset map to find the likely destination of Portuguese slave ships:

Map 93: Genomebiology.com reports that a large 2009 study found most black Americans came from the Yoruba and Manding tribal affiliations of West Africa. According to the map, which ports and 'coasts' did they most likely leave from?

_____

Pic(s) 94: Along with slaves, what else is seen In the hold of this slave ship on the right? _____	How many people were ships like these designed to hold? _____

Middle Passage

America Compared 95. Answer the Questions for Analysis below:

1)   2)

In a society without streetlights and patrol cars, why do you think the Chesapeake and South Carolina slave laws on things like running away were so harsh?	Graph 97: South Carolina's white population surpassed the black in 1785. For how many years did blacks remain the majority?

Thinking Like a Historian 98. Answer the 'Analyzing the Evidence' section:

1)

2)

3)

4)

5)

Pic 100: These images demonstrate: *a. cultural isolation*   *b. cultural diffusion*

Pic 101: These images indicate: *a. belief in natural rights*   *b. belief in Africans as property*

Stono Rebellion

What kinds of things were used as bribery by the Southern gentry to keep the yeoman farmers happy and win their votes?	Are these same kinds of bribery used today by politicians and parties to get people to vote for them? If so, what specific things are 'peddled?'

Gentility

Rate your gentility on a 1 (not at all) - 10 (I am the epitome of genteel) scale: _____

How many people did Philadelphia have in 1776, when upon the founding of the country it was the largest city in the land?	Does your city have more or less than that? _____ Depending on how you answered, what is the name of the city nearest to you which is opposite yours?

Map 104: Sketch out what was being sent on the triangular trade routes as shown on the map:

North America *Britain*
& the Caribbean

Africa

What kinds of jobs did laboring people tend to have in the maritime cities?

Men *Women*

Pic 105: What is notable about this painting according to the caption?	Hey if you could afford it, would you ever get an oil painting done of yourself or your family in the future? (it costs about $800 so you better save up!)

Salutary neglect

Patronage

Pic 107: Who is this guy and what did his motto *mean*, as in, what did he mean by it?

Besides being the most humorously named war in history (probably- but if you can find a weirder one then submit it to your teacher), the War of Jenkin's Ear, fought, and what was the outcome?

Molasses Act

When they say 'act', they often mean   a. tax   b. restriction   c. both of these

Land banks

American Voices 108. Answer the Questions for Analysis below:

1)

2)

3)

Pic 110: Why was the capture of Louisbourg both glorious and bittersweet for the British?

In Pic 110, you can see the British flag and naval ensign. Part of the ensign contains the Union Flag, dating from 1707 (rev. 1801) when England merged politically with Scotland. Compared with the flag you see here, the modern UK flag has an extra red cross, a thin one. It is St. Patrick's cross when Ireland was united with England and Scotland. The blue in the modern flag is St. Andrew's cross of Scotland, and the large red cross in both the one you see and the modern one is the Cross of St. George, a national symbol of England. Try to sketch it out below:

*Did you make it through without knowing the significace of Jacob Leisler or William Byrd II? If you did, then go find them and note it below. If you know them, move on to greener pastures.

Pg. 114 4 – GROWTH, DIVERSITY, AND CONFLICT Elect_____

"If you don't get your head-right and brush those teeth, you're going to get the kind of indenture that doesn't go away!" –Colonial Mom

Note the reasons Mr. MacAllister from the Highlands of Scotland gave to his friends for why North Carolina was the "best poor man's country":

| Pic 115: Describe a George Whitefield sermon: | Do you see evidence of any expressed emotion at this sermon? If so, what are the emotions? |

Tenants

Pic 116: Prudence _____'s painting packed a plethora of powerful pictures into a poignant progression of a person's puttering thorugh past, present and postmortem. Boom!

Competency

| Do you agree with the way inheritance was distributed in well-to-do families? | Do you agree with the way property changed hands during marriages? Why or why not? |

Thinking Like a Historian 26. Answer the 'Analyzing the Evidence' section:

1)

2)

3)

4)

Household mode of production

Map 120: St. George Manor made up a full one-half of this famous island: _____

Rensselaerswyck Manor contained the following present day cities:

Squatters

America Compared 121. Answer the Questions for Analysis below:

1)

2)

Chart 122: In 2013, the U.S. contained 41,200,000 immigrants. Divide the total as found on the chart of all the immigrants that came from 1700 to 1780 by that number to get the percentage: ___

| Pic 123: What do you think the 'Inner Light' is? | Pic 124: Was this kind of house common among German settlers or was it unique? |

Redemptioner

Map 125: Note the predominant ethnic groups in the following modern states:

Map 126: Note the predominant religious groups in the same states:

Massachusetts:

Connecticut:

Rhode Island:

New York:

Pennsylvania:

South Carolina:

North Carolina:

Virginia:

Enlightenment

Pietism

"Great Wagon Road"

Note the goals of the Enlightenment philosophers who carried on the work of Copernicus and Newton during the Scientific Revolution?

Natural rights

Benjamin Franklin

Deism

Pic 128: Philo=love of, anthropy='fellow man'. Why is this building called 'Enlightenment Philanthropy?

Pic 129: What does your new BFF (Ben Franklin's) suit say about him?

Franklin was a philosophical utilitarian. How does *Poor Richard's Almanack* illustrate that?

Revival

Johnathan Edwards

George Whitefield

American Voices 130. Answer the Questions for Analysis below:

1)

2)

3)

4)

Pic 132: Before the Internet and smartphones, there was TV and radio. Before that, the way to reach a wide audience that wasn't within hearing distance was by books and newspapers. If you were like Whitefield when writing this book, how specifically would *you* get your message out to as many people as possible?

Old Lights

New Lights

Great Awakening

Note some universities established originally by the religious enthusiasm of this era:

Graph 133: Which of the Christian denominations *more than doubled* from 1700 to 1780?

'Born Again' Christian

Describe briefly the claims of the French on the eve of the French and Indian War:	Describe briefly the claims of the Iroquois on the eve of the French and Indian War:
What happened at Fort Duquesne when young George Washington arrived there?	Map 136. Note the names of the major forts: *French* *British*

Tanaghrisson

Albany Plan

William Pitt and Lord Halifax in the British Parliament were called "war hawks". What did this mean and how did they convince the Prime Minister to declare war despite a large debt?

Pic 138: Why was George Washington not proud of his and General Edward Braddock's men at this engagement?

| What was William Pitt's war strategy?

James Wolfe

Map 139: List the year and winner of the important battles of the French and Indian War:

Siege of Fort Necessity _____ _____

Battle of Fort Duquesne _____ _____

Battle of Ft. Ticonderoga _____ _____

Battle of Louisbourg _____ _____

Battle of Ft. Frontenac _____ _____

Siege of Quebec _____ _____

Battle of Montreal _____ _____

Pontiac's Rebellion

Proclamation of 1763

Pic 140: What symbol of the *source* of Boylston's wealth is seen in this painting?

| Graph 141. Note two major things that increased during the Industrial Revolution around 1770:

Consumer revolution

Summarize the objectives and actions of the following:

The Paxton Boys *The Regulators*

Objectives:

Actions:

Pg. 150 — 5 – THE PROBLEM OF EMPIRE — Libertarian

"So, there is this shipment of tea due in from India soon, want to…"

Note why it was so important that Washington arrive at New York before William Tryon:

Pic 151: The cause of the Great New York Fire of 1776 was:

   a. The British   b. The Patriots   c. Unknown

Note how the following thought about "America" in the wake of victory in the F & I War:

Henry Ellis	Lord Halifax	John Dickinson

Note three strategies used by the British Parliament to raise money to pay the new debt burden imposed by the large-scale spending to win the French and Indian War:

1)

2)

3)

'Monied interests'

If "15 royal battalions" = 7,500 troops, how many soldiers are in a battalion?

Why were so many [Redcoat] British soldiers sent to be stationed in the Colonies at this point?

America Compared 153. Answer the Questions for Analysis below:

1)

2)

Map 154: Note the colonial power in control of the following modern day countries in 1770:

Eastern Canada and America: Brazil and Swahili Coast cities:

Mexico and the Philippines: Bengal and Madras India:

Andean South America: Sumatra, Java and the Moluccas:

Graph 155: You might have heard of the Malthusian dilemma, in which population grows faster than food supply and a crisis appears causing mass starvation and social chaos. You might have heard of hyperinflation, whereby money loses its value very quickly because so much of it is printed that each individual dollar (or whatever currency) becomes less valuable in relation to the goods and services it purchases. You might have heard of runaway greenhouse effect, a hypothetical situation whereby excess carbon dioxide and other gases coat the earth with a blanket that traps more and more sunlight and heat, and we wind up getting cooked. All crazy? Well, the first one happened on Easter Island, the second one happened recently in Zimbabwe, and the third happened on Venus. So what about the consequences of runaway government spending? From this graph, summarize the reasons for runaway spending in the era before social programs existed:

_____

George Grenville _____

Currency Act _____

Sugar Act _____

Vice-admiralty courts _____

Stamp Act _____

Virtual representation _____

Map 156: The British government *encouraged* *discouraged* colonials from settling west, past the Proclamation Line.

Quartering Act _____

How were Grenville's reforms similar to James II's declaration of the Dominion of New England nearly 100 years earlier?

_____

Patrick Henry _____

Stamp Act Congress _____

What was it about the Stamp Act specifically, that angered colonists in a way the Sugar and other acts only agitated them?

_____

Sons of Liberty _____

Pic 158: Describe some of the things the Sons of Liberty and others did to protest the new taxes:

English common law _____

Writ of Assistance _____

"Natural rights" _____

If you were a lawyer arguing both sides of the following, note your chief arguments:

Dickinson is right, people are slaves if they are taxed without their consent	*Dickinson is wrong, people are not slaves just because they are taxed without their consent*

Declaratory Act _____

Pic 160: Phillis Wheatley's story demonstrates that slavery was only a Southern phenomenon:	Chart 160: The minister friendliest to colonial aspirations was:
a. True b. False	_____ while _____ was the least.

Charles Townshend _____

Townshend Act _____

Revenue Act _____

Nonimportation movement _____

Daughters of Liberty _____

Pic 162: The cartoonist here is   a. supporting   b. ridiculing   the Edenton ladies' boycott.

Map 163: The city that saw the largest growth in troops deployments was _____.

Two southern cities that obtain new troop deployments were:	If you were in the military and stationed in a colony of your country, would you expect them to pay for your housing and food?

Thinking Like a Historian 26. Answer the 'Analyzing the Evidence' section:

1)

2)

3)

4)

Lord North

Boston Massacre

Pic 167: Note some of the consequences of the Boston Massacre:

Political: *Economic:*   *Social:*

_____   _____   _____

Graph 166: Trade was used as a political weapon in the form of boycotts on the American side, and levying or abolishing taxes on the British side. Today, the U.S. trade deficit with Mexico is ~45,000,000,000 per year. If that figure were on the chart in the book, the top of the chart would be around:
        a. as high as the whole book   b. taller than the school you are in right now

Committees of Correspondence

Tea Act

Coercive Acts

Why did the colonists brand the Coercive Acts 'Intolerable'?

Rate yourself 1-10. I would not cooperate with taxes I considered unfair or 'intolerable', like the colonists of old:	Today, taxes are higher than at any time in American history. Do you think there could be a taxpayer revolt or boycott in the future?

Continental Congress

Pic 169. Describe what happened at the Boston Tea Party:

Map 170: What modern state was almost called Transylvania?	How come the New England Protestants were all bent out of shape about the Proclamation of 1763?

Continental Association

Chart 171: Copy the British actions as a timeline on the left with the Patriot response on the right:

1762
1763
1764
1765
1766
1767
1768
1769
1770
1771
1772
1773
1774
1775
1776

American Voices 172. Answer the Questions for Analysis below:

1)

2)

3)

Loyalist

Neutral

Note the following about Dunmore's War:

Causes: *Course:* *Results:*

Map 175: Name the Indian tribes in the disputed green area into which settlers had come:

Patriots

Minutemen

Ever heard the story of the Midnight Ride of Paul Revere? At Old North Church in Boston, a historical landmark today, Revere conspired with the sexton who worked at the church to light one lantern in the steeple as a signal to the Patriots that the Redcoats were marching by land, and to light two if they were crossing over the river- 'by sea'- and assembling on the other shore before moving out to Lexington and Concord. He waited and got the signal- two lanterns. They shined for less than a minute, so the British would not think anything of it if they noticed. Revere and two others were off to warn the Minutemen and everyone else on the way to Lexington and Concord beyond, that

    A. *Hey y'all can go stain some silver or go back to bed y'all*   B. *The British are coming!*

Second Continental Congress

How did Lord Dunmore use promises to blacks and white servants to get them to join the Loyalist cause? | Pic 176: How did King George III feel about taxing the colonies?
|
|

Daniel Boone

Pic 177: Aside from the woman on horseback recalling Mary, what else about Bingham's portrait of Boone and his crew seems Biblical?

Olive Branch Petition

Popular sovereignty

Pic 178: Summarize the revolutionary Enlightenment ideas in documents written by the following:
        Thomas Paine   **Thomas Jefferson**

Pg. 182   **6 – MAKING WAR AND REPUBLICAN GOVERNMENTS**   Patriot_____

Don't start writing 'till you see the whites of the blanks where answers should be.

Pic 183: Check out the buttons on Washington's coat, and how wavy it is. There is something special about those attributes not taught about in the textbooks, at least not the ones used in government schools. Back when Washington was a 'Redcoat,' in 1755 during the French and Indian War, those buttons saved his life. General Braddock and Washington's men were ambushed from the trees, the exact same tactics the Patriots would use in the Revolutionary War, and Washington was moving across the battlefield relaying Braddock's orders. He was shot at by a hail of musket fire. Then again, and again and again. In fact, every other mounted officer was killed in the flurry of the ambush *except* Washington. Now, he had two horses shot out from under him, but he remounted each time and continued the battle, though a primary target the entire time. Over 700 men fell to their deaths all around him, but by some amazing circumstance, Washington survived. He wrote to his brother John, "I had been protected beyond all human probability or expectation; for I had four bullets through my coat, and two horses shot under me, yet escaped unhurt, although death was leveling my companions on every side." Later, and unbeknownst to Washington, the gold seal he wore on his uniform, which bore his initials of GW, was found. Why was it on the ground? It had a bullet hole through it.

What are those documents tattered on the ground at Washington's feet?

_____

Summarize the British versus the American forces as they were arrayed at the outset of the Revolution:

British   *American*

_____

William Howe _____

Battle of Long Island _____

Christmas, 1776 _____

Gentleman John Burgoyne _____

Battle of Saratoga _____

Pic 186: What were the results of the Battle of Princeton?	Pic 187: When Joseph Brant translated the Bible into Mohawk, this was an example of a. cultural diffusion b. assimilation c. both
Pic 188: Why were Patriot army soldiers dressed in such different clothes than the uniform British forces?	Pic 189: Virginia was beset by this after the war a. deflation b. inflation

Note some of the things that were causes of the loss of morale among the Patriots:

Valley Forge

Baron von Steuben

What were the motivations for the French-Patriot alliance?

Philipsburg Proclamation

Lord Cornwallis

Horatio Gates

Marquis de Lafayette

Comte de Rochambeau

Map 191: Describe George Rogers Clark's accomplishment for the Patriots:	If you were accompanying Clark on his trip west from Redstone Old Fort, note the rivers you'd have crossed:

Thinking Like a Historian 192. Answer the 'Analyzing the Evidence' section:

1)

2)

3)

Map 194: Put the six major battles in the South in chronological order on this timeline:

| 1777 | 1778 | 1779 | 1780 | 1781 |

Francis Marion

Battle of Yorktown

Despite being at a clear disadvantage at the start of the war, the American Patriots won. Why?

Currency tax

Treaty of Paris

If you were tasked with creating new institutions, what kind of overall political philosophy would you use as their foundation?

America Compared 197. Answer the Questions for Analysis below:

1)

2)

Pennsylvania constitution

What did John Adams warn people about when reacting to the Pennsylvania constitution?	Pic 199: Note reasons women like J.M. Murray argued for a different social status:

Mixed government

Graph 198: Do you think the people who own property would make better decisions than people who don't? If you were deciding which people in society should be able to vote, what requirements would you put on them? Should 10 year olds vote? You pick:

Summarize why the authors argue the following were 'losers' in the Revolutionary War:

Loyalists   *Native Americans*   *Slaves*

Articles of Confederation

Northwest Ordinance

Map 202: Why do you the various land claims states like Virginia and Georgia had were an indication of the weakness of the Articles of Confederation?

Pic 203: Sketch the blue township at right and follow the numerical pattern for each section:	Sketch he green section box and label the acrage:

Shay's Rebellion

Who were primary members of the nationalist faction and want did they want to accomplish?	Pic 205: What was Madison's major work?

Virginia Plan

New Jersey Plan

"Great Compromise"

What was 'ironic' about the argument on whether slaves should count in the tallying up of congressional delegates?

Federalists

Antifederalists

The Federalist

Imaging going back in time and sitting at the convention. Do you think you would favor the Federalists or Antifederalists more? Why?

American Voices 208. Answer the Questions for Analysis below:

1)

2)

3)

Federalist #10

Map 210: Who was more likely to favor ratification of the new Constitution?

    a. city folk   a. wealthy people

    b. country folk   b. poorer people

Note the states in which a majority in each district favored ratification:

If you were a lawyer arguing both sides of the case, note the arguments you'd use:

        Strong government is good   *Strong government is bad*

Pg. 214 — **7 – HAMMERING OUT A FEDERAL REPUBLIC** — Delegate _____

People have the right to have rights. I think.

What did Leopold von Ranke mean by his advice to the King of Bavaria?	When Washington left public life voluntarily after his second term as president, why did this 'astonish' people in Europe?

Pic 215: Note some American symbols in this painting:

John Adams

Judiciary Act

Bill of Rights

The Bill of Rights has been hailed as Jefferson and the Antifederalists' greatest achievement after the Revolution itself. Why? How did the Bill of Rights embody their political philosophy?

Report on the Public Credit

Alexander Hamilton

Graph 215: Hamilton established a permanent national debt. What was his rationale?	Not only Thomas Jefferson but Patrick Henry spoke out against Hamilton's plan. What was Mr. "Give me Liberty or give me death's" rationale against Hamilton?

Bank of the United States

Report on Manufactures

Pic 218: Contrast the two visions for America:

Hamilton's vision of a manufacturing colossus	*Jefferson's vision of an agrarian Republic*

Wealth of Nations

Proclamation of Neutrality

French Revolution

Jacobins

Whiskey Rebellion

John Jay

Thinking Like a Historian 221. Answer the 'Analyzing the Evidence' section:

1)

2)

3)

4)

5)

Jay's Treaty

Pic 222: What was the fate of the rebels who were arrested by Federal forces during the Whiskey Rebellion?

Haitian Revolution

Pic 223: Why did some Americans find the Haitian Revolution a 'perversion of Republican values?'

XYZ Affair

Naturalization Act

Alien Act

Sedition Act

America Compared 224. Answer the Questions for Analysis below:

1)

2)

Virginia and Kentucky Resolutions

Why did Jefferson consider the election of 1800 to be 'revolutionary?'

Map 225 (top): Generalize about the geographic divide in the 1796 election:	What does it mean that candidates and political strategists began making 'mental maps' of the field?

Map 225 (bot.): What does it mean that New York was the 'pivotal swing state' in the 1800 election?

What did the following recommend be done with the American Indians?

William Henry Drayton   *Henry Knox*

Western Confederacy

Mad Anthony Wayne

Battle of Fallen Timbers

Treaty of Greenville

Map 227: How might forming territorial governments in the Midwest and Cotton Belt help 'legitimize' the Euro-American hold on these territories and 'delegitimize' Indian 'ownership' of the land?

How did the following Indian religious men go about reconciling (or not reconciling) their tribes to white-American ways?

Handsome Lake	*Red Jacket*

Pic 228: How did the artist convey a sense of equality between the whites and the Indians?	Map 229: What 'four cultures' had emerged in America by 1790?
	1) 2)
	3) 4)

Map 229: If beginning in the following place, which future states would a person most likely be migrating to?

New England:

Mid-Atlantic:

Chesapeake:

Lower South:

Cotton gin

Pic 230: Do you think the adoption of new technology (in this case of construction design) is a universal good, or does it ruin the cultural ways of a people like these Chickasaws?	Note the agricultural innovations on the eastern farms in this era:

Marbury v. Madison

Jefferson was a war hawk, ready to entangle in international alliances: *a. true   b. false*

Pic 232: What city (not far from Benghazi) was the focus on America's intervention shown here? _____

Name the major American warship that won: _____

Barbary 'piracy' was raiding the Spanish, Italian and other coasts looking for villagers to capture as slaves, and extortion. How did Jefferson respond to these states' demands for tribute?

_____

Louisiana Purchase _____

Aaron Burr _____

Lewis & Clark _____

Sacagawea _____

Pic 234: Why did the Mandan village have a wall if white settlers were not yet in this area?

_____

***Chesapeake* incident** _____

Embargo Act _____

Tecumseh _____

William Henry Harrison _____

Map 235: Population density was greatest here in 1803:
    a. The Northeast   *b. The Midwest*

Both Lewis & Clark and Pike began their travels in this city with a famous arch: _____

Battle of Tippecanoe _____

Pic 236: What did the term 'holy war' mean for Tenskwatawa?

_____

War of 1812 _____

Oliver Hazard Perry _____

Battle of Lake Erie _____

1-10: How surprised are you to learn that Washington D.C. was burned down in war? _____

Pic 237: What is the 'grain of truth' in this propaganda art that made it so convincing?

American Voices 238. Answer the Questions for Analysis below:

1)

2)

3)

4)

Map 240: Follow the course of the War of 1812, noting the geographic location of the key events in case you are in any of these states in the future and want to visit the battlefield site:

	Event	*Winner of the Day*	*Modern state in which event took place*
1			
2			
3			
4			
5			
6			
7			
8			
9			
10			

Treaty of Ghent

Henry Clay

Second Bank of the United States

John Marshall

McCulloch v. Maryland

Chart 242: Reorder this chart as indicated below:

Case Year Issue at Hand and Significance

Of all these trials, which would you pick to witness firsthand because the issue at hand seems most interesting to you? (yes you have to pick one, do NOT write 'none of them'... or else... :)

James Monroe

John Quincy Adams

Adams-Onis Treaty

Monroe Doctrine

"Era of Good Feelings"

Map 244: Sketch a freehand map of the U.S. and label the major divisions, labeling each:

Pg. 248 — 8 – CREATING A REPUBLICAN CULTURE — Citizen_____

Federalist: "Everyone come to Washington D.C. for a meeting." Antifederalist: "Let's just Skype this meeting. Seriously. We don't need to go there."

What amazing coincidence was ascribed by many white Americans to divine intervention as they looked back on their recent successes in designing effective institutions?

_____

Pic 249: The moral mission these and many American women undertook was part of the Second Great Awakening. What was that?

_____

'Neomercantilism'

John Jacob Astor

Pic 250: If you saw a dude walking around your grocery store in this outfit, how would you react?

_____

How did Jeffersonians feel about the existence of a national bank that was really a private company?	What happened to the Bank in 1811?

Pic 251: In the China trade, what was traded?

From China to USA →   ←*From USA to China*

_____

Panic of 1819

Thinking Like a Historian 26. Answer the 'Analyzing the Evidence' section:

1)

2)

3)

4)

Pic 254: Why is the image selected here an apt depiction of American economics in this era?

___

Draw each of the new forms of transportation in your own way and label it:

Turnpike   *Canal*

___

Commonwealth System

___

What did the Polish aristocrat mean when he commented on American society being different than European?

___

Map 257 (left): In 1800, what did a white man usually have to 'do' in order to vote? | Map 257 (right): In 1830, what did a white man have to 'do' in most states in order to be allowed to vote?

___

Sentimentalism

___

Companionate marriage

___

Demographic transition

___

Republican motherhood

___

Pic 259: How did republican ideals, the new economic circumstances and cultural values affect marriages?

___

American Voices 260. Answer the Questions for Analysis below:

1)

2)

3)

4)

Contrast the different kinds of parenting styles in early-19th century America:

Permissive   *Developmental*   *Authoritarian*

The Three 'Rs'

Pic 263: What subject are these girls studying? _____

How did the book *The Life of George Washington* help American kids learn about values?

Noah Webster

Washington Irving

Pic 264: Why did many people feel strange about the existence of a slave system in a country built on the idea of freedom? | Map 265: These states opted for gradual abolition of slavery:

Manumission

Herrenvolk republic

American Colonization Society

Liberia

How did the ACS plan to organize the transports of so many people out of the country? Were they successful?

Pg. 276: There is a big debate about buildings like this on college campuses. Drayton had the building designed and built with earnings he received as a plantation owner using slave labor. In your opinion, should 'Drayton Hall' have its name changed because of this history? Why or why not?

Missouri Compromise

Map 269: The major division in the country that the Missouri Compromise- well executed as it was- intensified, was the division between these geographic regions: | What 'new state' was admitted to 'balance' Missouri's admission?

Established church

Voluntarism

'Unchurched'

Second Great Awakening

Graph 271: The two major denominations of the Christian religion that pulled ahead of the others in this time were the following:
   1)   2)

America Compared 14. Answer the Questions for Analysis below:

1)

2)

How was black Christianity different than that of the white population?

Unitarians

Map 273: The two hearths of the Second Great Awakening were:

          Hearth   Path of diffusion
1)

2)

Pic 274: What do the authors say is exaggerated in this painting from 1839? | In what ways did women respond to the Second Great Awakening?

How did Emma Willard help women gain a religious and/or educational footing?

Pg. 284 9 – TRANSFORMING THE ECONOMY **Know-Something**_____
Provide your answers in Morse Code for extra credit* *At U.S. Military Academy only

How come Waterbury, CT became the clockmaking center of the U.S. and an example of the entrepreneurial culture? | Pic 285: Note the tools the girls shown here are posing with:
_____

Industrial Revolution

Division of labor

The process described by Frederick Law Olmstead might be kind of gross but is also:

    a. time-consuming   *b. efficient*

Graph 286: In which industries did workers add the most value to the products they were producing? Why were there workers more 'productive' than others?

Mineral-based economy

Cyrus McCormick

Mechanics

Contrast American and British advantages in early industry:

    British   *American*

Francis Cabot Lowell

Waltham-Lowell System

Map 288: The area where cotton was produced into textiles was primarily

    a. the Northeast   *b. the Midwest*   *c. The South*   *d. the Great West*

America Compared 14. Answer the Questions for Analysis below:

1)

2)

Machine tools

Pic 290: If you hang around people doing cool stuff like Whitney was, it has an effect on you. who did he affect in real life to do his own inventing?

| At the Crystal Palace exhibition, what kinds of American products were on display?

Unions

Pic 292: This woodworker, it says, is showing his pride. What evidence can you see that supports that statement?

Commonwealth v. Hunt

Labor theory of value

Market Revolution

Erie Canal

Map 294: "Go west young man, go west," was a sign visible on many a storefront window in eastern cities. The biggest states or territories in land sales in the period 1830-39 were:

| Pic 295: The Erie Canal had something to do with the spike in land sales
|
| a. T   b. F

Robert Fulton

Cleremont

Map 296: Describe the three great transportation system in mid-19th century America:

1)   2)   3)

John Deere

Map 297: The railroad hub of the South was _____, in the Midwest it was _____

Thinking Like a Historian 298. Answer the 'Analyzing the Evidence' section:

1)

2)

3)

4)

5)

Map 300: What made St. Louis, Cincinnati, Louisville and Nashville connected in an urban system?	Do you think the descendants of people in CT and RI should issue a written apology for what their ancestors did in the 1800s?
Describe the American agrarian social order with regards to how people dressed and could tell each other apart in wealth	How did the onset of the Industrial Age change all that?

Middle class

Pic 302: How can you tell these are elite and not middle class people?	Did you catch that reparations thing earlier from the people in Rhode Island and CT? It was for this activity. What were the positives and negatives of this activity?

Describe the American work ethic as Franklin did in his *Autobiography*:

Pic 304: Do you believe that if you work hard enough you could afford a house like the one shown? How about in the past?

Self-made man

The lot of the poor Americans was worse than that of the middle class and elite. Describe how:

Benevolent Empire

Negro Election Day

Sabbatarian values

Pic 306: What was Finney known for?

What did Finney mean when he said God made all people 'moral free agents?'

Note some of the reasons for the rise of the Temperance Movement:

Pic 307: List the steps of the *Drunkard's Progress,* the most famous alcohol-related comic:

Step 1   Step 2   Step 3   Step 4   Step 5   Step 6   Step 7   Step 8   Step 9

American Voices 308. Answer the Questions for Analysis below:

1)

2)

3)

American Temperance Society

Nativist

Pg. 314 10 – A DEMOCRATIC REVOLUTION Bankster_____

*"I... killed... the bank!" -President Andrew Jackson; his last words before he died, when asked about his **greatest** accomplishment.*

Draw a Venn Diagram comparing and contrasting how Frances Trollope described the *Domestic Manners of the Americans* in 1832 vs. how Alexis de Tocqueville did in *Democracy in America*:

Pic 315: "Stump speaking" was a major theme of the 2016 election year, as Trump, Clinton and Sanders all drew crowds and 'played to the people.' What do you think this term means in the context of a political speech?

_____

Franchise

Notables

Political machine

America Compared 317. Answer the Questions for Analysis below:

1)

2)

_____

Spoils system

Caucus

American System

Internal improvements

Pic 318: Describe Martin Van Buren's characteristics:

Map 319: Why was the 1824 election so contested?

Corrupt bargain

Consolidated government

Pic 320: What did the Tariff of Abominations do to motivate the cartoonist to draw this?

John C. Calhoun

Andrew Jackson

How did various people describe Andrew Jackson's 'Democracy'?

Thomas Morris   *English Observer*   *Daniel Webster*

Graph 322: Describe the changes in percentage of people voting in elections as shown here:	Map 322: Which section of the country voted for J.Q. Adams?

Kitchen Cabinet

'Rotation'

Pic 323: How did Jackson's political philosophy differ from Hamilton and Clay's?

Tariff of 1828

Nullification

Do you think a state should be able to nullify a federal law that the state believes is unconstitutional *or* not in its best interests? Why or why not?	How did South Carolina justify nullification on constitutional grounds?

States' rights

Pic 324: How did the "Little Magician" figure into the election of 1832?	Pic 325: How did the following argue in this Senate debate?
	Hayne *Webster*

The Bank War

Second Bank of the United States

Nicholas Biddle

Characterize the Bank of the United States (a *private* corporation despite its name, though partially owned by the U.S. government) in the 1830s.

Its good aspects	*Why people distrusted it and Biddle*

Did Henry Clay's pressing of the Bank charter issue for the 1832 election work or did it backfire?

While Congress voted to recharter the Bank, Jackson knew many had been paid off in order to vote that way and vetoed it. He wanted American money back in regular state banks, and backed by precious metals to limit money printing and inflation. But the Bank still had four years on its existing charter, so he vowed to the people to "destroy the monster". He called the Bank that because of its large foreign ownership and potential to put a stranglehold on the U.S. economy (and with it, in his view, U.S. independence). But now Biddle (the equivalent of a Fed chairman) and 'his' Bank, supported by the international banking community, went 'to war' with Jackson! How did Biddle use the Bank to try and cause financial distress in American in order to make the President submit?

If you were a lawyer arguing both sides, how would you defend the following propositions?

The Cherokees were integrated into American society	*The Cherokees maintained a separate culture*

Indian Removal Act

Pic 327: This chief's name is   *a. Red Jacket*   *b. Blackhawk*

American Voices 328. Answer the Questions for Analysis below:

1)

2)

3)

Map 330: Note the general direction of each tribe's removal:

Choctaw _____   *Creek* _____   *Chickasaw* _____   *Seminole* _____

Cherokee _____   This tribe was transported across the Gulf of Mexico _____

The 'Trail of Tears' route of the Cherokee took them past this Tennessee city _____

Indian Territory

Note the decisions in the following cases:

Cherokee Nation v. Georgia   *Worcester v. Georgia*

Pic 331: What was the purpose of depicting this scene?

Trail of Tears

Winfield Scott

"As the United States was a 'White Man's Country,' Indian Territory was to be a 'Red Man's Country." What did this statement mean for Indians who were part black?

Roger B. Taney

How did the Taney court decide in the following cases:

Charles River Bridge Co. v. Warren Bridge Co.:

Dartmouth College v. Woodward:

Mayor of N.Y. v. Miln:

Briscoe v. Bank of Kentucky:

Classical liberalism (Laissez-faire)

Whigs

Pic 333: Describe Calhoun's social philosophy:

Anti-Masons

Working-Men's Parties

Panic of 1837

Pic 335: What evidence of 'hard times' do you see in this picture?

Thinking Like a Historian 336. Answer the 'Analyzing the Evidence' section:

1)

2)

3)

4)

5)

Specie Circular

John Tyler

Ethnocultural politics

Pg. 344 **11 – RELIGION AND REFORM** **Transcendentalist**_____

No, you are not allowed to Missouri Compromise your way out of doing half this assignment.

In what social spheres does the 'laborer with a family' say reform should take place in c. 1842?	Pic 345: Which items in this painting are depictive of romantic love?

Individualism

American Renaissance

Transcendentalism

Pic 346: Describe some of Emerson's key thoughts which impacted American culture:

Describe the contributions of the following people Emerson influenced:

Henry David Thoreau   *Margaret Fuller*   *Walt Whitman*

Pic 348: Describe Fuller's sad fate in the end: _____

Note the influence of the 'darker visions' of the following:

Nathanial Hawthorne   *Herman Melville*

Utopias

Shakers

Mother Ann

Map 349: Most Shaker communities were located in this part of the country: _____

Pic 350: Why did Americans view Shakers with suspicion? | The Shakers celibacy meant no future Shakers. Are they around anymore?
| *a. yes*   *b. no*

Fourierism

Socialism

Albert Brisbane

Oneida community

Pic 351: Note two ways this image depicts a 'role-reversal' of the sexes of the time:

Perfectionism

Mormonism

Joseph Smith

Brigham Young

Pic 352: How does this image illustrate 'plural celestial marriage'? | Map 353: Starting at Fayette, NY, note the states the Mormons passed through in order on the trek to Utah:

Draw and label lines tracing the population of each of the following cities in the following times:
New York, Philadelphia

```
1,000,000   |
            |
  750,000   |
            |
  500,000   |
            |
  250,000   |
            |
        0   |
            _____
            1800                  1840                  1860
```

Describe the number, origin, and average age of prostitutes in New York City in 1855: | Pic 355: What kind of change in the culture of urban America does this scene demonstrate?

Minstrelsy

Graph 356: What two factors contributed to heavy immigration to America in the 1840s and early-1850s? | How come immigration slowed in the late-1850s and 1860s?

Nativist movement

Pic 357: Do you think it is offensive to spell standard English language words in a way that sound phonetically like a group of people who don't speak RP (received pronunciation) speak the language? | Have you ever done so in a text message or email?

Thinking Like a Historian 358. Answer the 'Analyzing the Evidence' section:

1)

2)

3)

4)

Abolitionist

'Uplift'

Pic 360: What did Walker appeal for?

Nat Turner

William Lloyd Garrison

Note the writers and content of the following abolitionist treatises:

Genius of Universal Emancipation   *Immediate, not Gradual Abolition*

The Bible Against Slavery   *Slavery as It Is*

Underground Railroad

Fugitive Slave Law

Map 363: Why did most former slaves who used the Underground Railroad go to the specific places- remote Northern towns- they did?

Harriet Tubman

Harriet Tubman was chosen by the Obama Administration in 2016 to replace Andrew Jackson on the $20 dollar bill a few years from now. If you had been on the committee deciding this change, how would you have voted and why?

Pic 364: How do the pictures shown help illustrate Josiah Priest's argument that slavery was a 'positive good' for Africans brought to America?

Amalgamation

Gag rule

| Pic 365: How does this scene depict the fear of racial amalgamation on the part of the cartoonist? | Pic 366: What are the family members doing in this picture?

'Separate sphere'

Dorothea Dix

Horace Mann

Catharine Beecher

American Voices 368. Answer the Questions for Analysis below:

1)

2)

3)

Harriet Beecher Stowe

Angelina Grimke

Domestic slavery

Chart 370: The state with the highest volume of antislavery action was:	Most antislavery activists were
_____	a. men b. women c. both

Pic 371: Note the contributions to reform of the following:

Elizabeth Cady Stanton   *Susan B. Anthony*

Married women's property laws

Seneca Falls Convention

America Compared 372. Answer the Questions for Analysis below:

1)

2)

Pg. 376 | **12 – THE SOUTH EXPANDS** | **Freedman_____**

Wait, so that was all real?

How was it that the boast could be made in 1840 that 'Cotton is King'?

Pic 377: Is there a Dalmatian dog laying down sideways in this picture or is that just cotton?

Graph 378: Note where, in each of the following years, the most cotton was being produced:

1800:   1820:   1840:   1860:

1810:   1830:   1850:

Map 379: As a general directional trend, describe the settlement of the slave population over time:

_____

Coastal trade _____

Inland system _____

Pic 381: Why did the Chesapeake tidewater economy benefit from the slave trade when most of the new transports of slaves were going to wind up south and west of that area?

_____

Chattel principle _____

Pic 382: Are these slaves being sold as individuals or in families?

a. as individuals   b. in families   c. both

Pic 383: What about this building clues you in that it was done in a 'Greek-revival' style?

Benevolent masters _____

American Voices 384. Answer the Questions for Analysis below:

1)

2)

3)

4)

5)

Republican aristocracy

What do you think the following statements by Southern landed aristocrats actually meant?

'Inequality is the law of the universe'	'The sovereign people, alias mob...'

America Compared 387. Answer the Questions for Analysis below:

1)

2)

'Positive good'

Gang-labor system

Slave society

Pic 390: The overall message here in this painting by Beard is: a. optimistic   b. pessimistic

Stephen F. Austin

In 1835, there were about 9 times more   a. Americans   b. Mexicans   living in Tejas (Texas).

Sam Houston

What did General Antonio de Santa Ana do in 1835 that angered the American-Texans, and how did the American-Texans react in 1836?

Alamo

Davy Crockett & Jim Bowie

Pic 392: What were the aspirations of the American-Texans in this painting? | Map 393: The key victory of the Texas over Mexican forces in the battle for independence occurred at:

Secret ballot

Pic 394: How does this image capture reasons Southern planters were not interested in big cities or industrialization?

Black Protestantism

How did Charles C. Jones describe the spiritual beliefs of Africans in America in 1842? | Pic 396: This painting depicts slaves dancing at a celebration in 1838. It reflects more of:

 a. assimilation   b. cultural diversity

Gullah dialect

Task system

Thinking Like a Historian 398. Answer the 'Analyzing the Evidence' section:

1)

2)

3)

4)

Pic 400: Compare the slave quarters here to the Texans' quarters on pg. 392. Given the choice, where would you prefer to live and why? | Pic 401: Scan the names shown here. How many would you consider to be 'common' names today? How many not?

 Common _____

 Uncommon _____

Note two key differences between the lives of African Americans in the North and the South:

Pg. 410 **13 – EXPANSION, WAR AND SECTIONAL CRISIS** **Pioneer**_____

You must transcend the limitations of your mind and become one with the stream of history, for as a river flows, so flows the river of time. -Yoda

Note the quotes by the following sources on American destiny:

New York Evening-Post   *Francis Baylies*

President James Polk   *Thomas Hart Benton*

Pic 411: What symbols of American progress does *Liberty* carry with her? | What symbols elsewhere in the painting continue the themes of advancing forth?

For what political reason was the question of slavery to 'rip the nation apart'?

Manifest Destiny

According to John O'Sullivan, what was the destiny of the following peoples:

Americans   *Native Americans and Mexicans*

'Oregon fever'

Map 412: The Willamette Valley, where most people who traveled the Oregon Trail settled, is located south of this city: | Pic 413: The settlers who came to Oregon were careful to
|
| a. assimilate to native ways   b. keep their culture

Map 414: Start at the beginning of each of the following trails. Use dots as places and lines for rivers, labeling the places the Conestoga wagons of the settlers crossed to get to their destinations:

Ft. Vancouver   Mormon-California Trail
                                                                   Nauvoo

Sacramento   Oregon Trail
                                                                   Independence

Californios

Pic 415: Aside from Conestoga wagons, what other kinds of things did the settlers have with them that stretched 'far as the eye could see'?	Pic 416: The tribe that ruled this area was:

What was the lifestyle of the following tribes of the Great West:

Comanches, Kiowa, Cheyennes and Arapahos:

Blackfeet: *Lakota-Souix:*

Native American marriage practices tended to be more like:

a. the polygamous societies of the Middle East and Africa   b. the monogamous society of America

Note the atmosphere in American politics before the fateful 1844 election:

The Dark Horse, James K. Polk, who came out of almost nowhere to win the presidency, began an expansionist program. Describe what he did:

54/40 or Fight!

John C. Fremont

John Slidell

Zachary Taylor

Trace the places attained by the following generals

   Winfield Scott:

   Zachary Taylor:

   Stephen Kearney:

Where did Commodore Sloat land after leaving Mazatlan to aid the rebels in California? _____

Bear Flag Republic

Pic 420: Describe the fighting in Monterrey, Mexico:	Which American general captured the Mexican capital and raised the U.S. flag over the capital building?

Conscious Whigs

Wilmot Proviso

Treaty of Guadeloupe Hidalgo

Why did John C. Calhoun not favor annexing all of Mexico but only the sparsely populated areas in the north?

Free-soil movement

American Voices 422. Answer the Questions for Analysis below:

1)

2)

3)

4)

Map 424: The modern state of Texas is   a. larger   b. smaller   than the old Republic of Texas.

The area south of the Gila River was added after the Mexican War by   a. conquest   b. purchase

What was the purpose that Gadsden and others pushed for the acquisition of this territory?

Squatter sovereignty

'49ers

Map 427: The following towns lay within the Gold Rush region:

a. San Francisco   b. Sutter's Mill   c. Stockton   d. Sacramento

On this map, what is San Francisco labeled as? _____

Why are there no purple bars on the inset graph in the years 1849-1851?

America Compared 426. Answer the Questions for Analysis below:

1)

2)

Pic 428: Mariano Vallejo wrote the following after the Bear Flag Republic was declared, when he was asked why many *Californios* fought the Americans who raised it:

"If the men who hoisted the 'Bear Flag' had raised the flag that Washington sanctified by his abnegation and patriotism, there would have been no war on the Sonoma frontier, for all our minds were prepared to give a brotherly embrace to the sons of the Great Republic, whose enterprising spirit had filled us with admiration. Ill-advisedly, however, as some say, or dominated by a desire to rule without let or hindrance, as others say, they placed themselves under the shelter of a flag that pictured a bear, an animal that we took as the emblem of rapine and force. This mistake was the cause of all the trouble, for when the Californians saw parties of men running over their plains and forests under the 'Bear Flag,' they thought that they were dealing with robbers and took the steps they thought most effective for the protection of their lives and property."

Which flag should Fremont and the Americans probably have raised to avoid the conflict?

    a. the Bear Flag   b. the American flag   c. the Spanish flag

'Slavery follows the flag'

Compromise of 1850

Map 429: Note the status conferred on the following Western territories by 'Clay's Compromise':

California and Oregon:

Utah and New Mexico:

Oklahoma:

Texas and Missouri:

Note the status conferred on Kansas and Nebraska by the Kansas-Nebraska Act of 1854:

Pic 430: Clay's great victory in attaining these compromises is that he

Who do you think benefitted more from its terms?

Uncle Tom's Cabin

Personal-liberty laws

Who won the election of 1852?

a. Lewis Cass   b. Winfield Scott   c. Stephan Douglas   d. Franklin Pierce

Gadsden Purchase

Ostend Manifesto

Kansas-Nebraska Act

American Party

Why were the American Party members called the 'Know Nothings'?

Bleeding Kansas

Dred Scott

Thinking Like a Historian 434. Answer the 'Analyzing the Evidence' section:

1)

2)

3)

4)

5)

Map 436: Did Lincoln win any of the Southern states in the 1860 election? _____

Pic 437: Lincoln might not be 'handsome' in the opinion of the authors, but he seems intimidating.

Freeport Doctrine

Pic 439: Lincoln is playing the proto-form of this sport _____

Pg. 444   14 – TWO SOCIETIES AT WAR   Free soiler _____

If you play your cards right and work hard right now, soon this chapter will be gone with the wind. Then, it's hammock time!

Note the way in which the following described what they saw in the Civil War:

    Elisha Hunt Rhodes   *R.M. Collins*   *Abraham Lincoln*

___

Pic 445: What was the costliest single day in American history- and how many died?

___

Pic 446: What does the star symbolize in this Alabama flag?	Map: 447: Note the states that seceded in order:			
	1)	2)	3)	
	4)	5)	6)	
	7)	8)	9)	10)

Crittenden Compromise

___

Robert E. Lee

___

If you were a lawyer arguing both sides, what would your arguments be defending the following:

Slave ownership was the primary reason for secession (see pie chart)	Other factors were primary in secession

If you were a lawyer arguing both sides, what would your arguments be defending the following:

South Carolina was just in seceding from the Union, after all, it was the same thing the 13 Colonies did	The Federal Government was right in asserting the "Union is perpetual"

Jefferson Davis _____

P.G.T. Beauregard _____

Battle of Manassas (Bull Run) _____

George McClellan _____

Stonewall Jackson _____

Map 450: Note the major battles, the generals involved, and the outcomes:

	Battle	*Generals*	*Outcome*
1			
2			
3			
4			
5			
6			
7			
8			
9			
10			

In your estimation, which side was most successful in the years 1861 and 1862? Why?

_____

Pic 451: Note the side of the image, left or right, and the colors worn by the following sides:

	Right or Left	*Color of Uniforms*
Union		
Confederacy		

Did Lincoln pick Hooker, Grant or Burnside to replace McClellan *first*? _____

David G. Farragut

Total war

Conscription

Map 453: Note the major battles, the generals involved, and the outcomes:

	Battle	Generals	Outcome
1			
2			
3			
4			
5			
6			
7			
8			
9			
10			
11			
12			

Habeas corpus

Militia Act of 1862

Pic 454: In modern times, are most American enlisted soldiers older or younger than the guys shown here?	Pic 455: How many days would it take the average worker to make the amount offered to sign up for the war in this pic?
Pic 456: What kinds of jobs did women have to supported the war effort?	Graph 457: Who had the advantage in this war according to this graph?

King Cotton

Pic 457: Note six things about the Confederate capital city that you see in this picture:

Thinking Like a Historian 458. Answer the 'Analyzing the Evidence' section:

1)

2)

3)

4)

Homestead Act of 1862

Greenbacks

In what ways did the policies of the Republican-controlled Congress of the Lincoln Administration redefine the character of the federal government?

America Compared 461. Answer the Questions for Analysis below:

1)

2)

Pic 462: Why is this Southern family homeless? | Pic 463: Why is this African-American family on the run?

Contrabands

Radical Republicans

Thaddeus Stevens

Emancipation Proclamation

Did Lincoln *want* to free the Southern slaves? Cite your evidence:	Which political party was most against freeing the slaves?

Map 465: Note the major battles, the generals involved, and the outcomes:

	Battle	Generals	Outcome
1			
2			
3			

Pic 467: What was unique about the 107th infantry unit of the Union Army?

William T. Sherman

Scorched-earth campaign

War Democrats

Peace Democrats

Map 469: Note the major battles, the generals involved, and the outcomes:

	Battle	Generals	Outcome
1			
2			
3			
4			
5			

6

7

8

Pic 470: Sherman said, "War is Hell." In your opinion, did he bring 'Hell' upon the South during the March to the Sea? Why or why not?

| Do you think Grant and Sherman's 'hard war' strategy was responsible for Northern victory?

Map 471: Note the major battles, the generals involved, and the outcomes:

	Battle	Generals	Outcome
1			
2			
3			
4			
5			
6			
7			
8			
9			
10			

American Voices 472. Answer the Questions for Analysis below:

1)

2)

3)

Pg. 478   **15 – RECONSTRUCTION**   **Yank/Reb**_____

Now these are such sad times / that we're all living in / for killing your brother / is the mightiest sin.   -Waylon Jennings

Pic 479: What was the 15th Amendment and who is shown celebrating it in this image?

_____

Ten Percent Plan

Wade-Davis Bill

John Wilkes Booth

Pic 480: What caused the Memphis Riot?

_____

Black Codes

Freedman's Bureau

Civil Rights Act of 1866

14th Amendment

America Compared 482. Answer the Questions for Analysis below:

1)

2)

_____

Reconstruction Act

Map 483: Place the eleven states of the former Confederacy in order of their overthrow of the Reconstructionist governments:

_____

Andrew Johnson

Ulysses S. Grant

Table 484: Note the key provision of the following laws:

13th Amendment

Civil Rights Act

14th Amendment

Reconstruction Act

Tenure of Office Act

15th Amendment

Ku Klux Klan Act

Pic 485: Aside from political cartoons, what famous figure did Thomas Nast help 'create'?	How did Elizabeth Cady Stanton feel about the enfranchisement of black males?

Pic 486: Who was left 'out in the cold' in the opinion of the cartoonist and why?

AWSA

NWSA

Minor v. Happersett

Which of the following groups of people would most likely send Thaddeus Stevens a thank you card and why?

Why?

a. White Southerners   b. Black Southerners

American Voices 472. Answer the Questions for Analysis below:

1)

2)

3)

Sharecropping

Pic 490: What evidence is there in this picture that this is a family of sharecroppers?

Map 491: What are the essential physical changes that the Barrow Plantation went through after the Civil War?

Why were federal troops required in many elections across the South between 1868 and 1871?

Union League

Scalawags

Carpetbaggers

Pic 494: What policies did Reconstruction legislators like Hiram Revels pursue?

Pic 495: Note three things that would have made this Freedman's school a better learning environment:

Convict leasing

Civil Rights Act of 1875

What did *The Prostrate State* by Pike claim about the Reconstruction governments?

Why didn't the North send troops to stop the Southern whites from ending Reconstruction?

Freedman's S&T Company

Pic 496: Name a famous Negro spiritual:

Pic 499: What was the goal of the white supremacists?

Classical liberalism

Laissez-faire

Horace Greeley

Credit Mobilier

'Redemption'

Nathan B. Forrest

Ku Klux Klan

Enforcement laws

How did the following view the end of Reconstruction?

Ex-Confederates	*Freedpeople*	*Republicans*	*Class. Liberals*

Slaughter-house cases

U.S. v. Cruikshank

Civil Rights Cases

Describe the following about the election of 1877:

Candidates and stances:

Why it was disputed:

The outcome:

Pic 501: What exactly is 'Grantism'?

Thinking Like a Historian 502. Answer the 'Analyzing the Evidence' section:

1)

2)

3)

4)

The 'Lost Cause'

British military historian John Keegan said he likes traveling to the American South today, because it is the 'only part of America defeated in war' on the territory of the present country. Do you think losing a war on your own territory does something to an individual or the collective psyche?

Pg. 505: Go back and note the significance of the following:

Charles Sumner

Robert Smalls

Blanche K. Bruce

Timeline 507: What important events happened in 1877 (besides Thomas Edison inventing the lighbulb?

Pg. 508   **16 – CONQUERING A CONTINENT**   **Granger**_____

What makes a nation's pillars high, and its foundations strong? What makes it mighty to defy, the foes that round it throng?
Not gold but only men can make, a people great and strong; Men who for truth and honor's sake, stand fast and suffer long.
Brave men who work while others sleep, who dare while others fly, they build a nation's pillars deep, and lift them to the sky. -Emerson

Transcontinental RR

Pic 509: What does this image depict about the Great West that would make *you* consider moving?

Protective tariff

Treaty of Kanagawa

| Did you think Cinco de Mayo was Mexico's independence day? It's not. What really happened on that day in 1867? | Pic 511: What's this ship doing in Yokohama? |

Burlingame Treaty

William Seward

While the Civil War left the nation in   *surplus*   *debt*   the tariff left it in   *surplus*   *debt*

Map 513: Most RR lines were located   *east*   *west*   of the Mississippi River.

America Compared 514. Answer the Questions for Analysis below:

1)

2)

Munn v. Illinois

Peones

Ejidos

Gold standard

'Crime of 1873'

Homestead Act

Morrill Act

Land-grant colleges

Comstock Lode

Map 517 (top): Note the following in the varying colors on this map:

        Cities   *Silver*   *Gold*

Pink

Tan

Brown

Map 517 (bot.): Which region shown saw the most growth between 1860 and 1891:	Pic 518: Note some characteristics of the following
	Real cowboys *Mythic cowboys*

Long Drive

'Rain follows the plow'

Homesteaders

'American fever'

Exodusters

Pic 520: What kind of environmental challenges did settlers like these face?

Emmeline Wells

John Wesley Powell

American Voices 522. Answer the Questions for Analysis below:

1)

2)

3)

Pic 524: What factors led to the creation of the first national parks like this one?

Pic 525: Were the buffalo hunted to extinction or not?

Yosemite

Yellowstone

U.S. Fisheries Commission

'Reservation wars'

Chief Joseph

Map 526: Place the eight battles shown here in chronological order

1   2

3   4

5   6

7   8

By 1890, the state with the most land devoted to Indian reservations was _____

Pic 527: One thing the Dakota Indians at Pike's island did not have to worry about was:

    a. local hostility   *b. cold weather*   *c. hot weather*

Sand Creek massacre

Fetterman massacre

Red Cloud

Natinal Indian Defense Association

Pic 529: Note three surprising things in Red Cloud's quarters:

Thinking Like a Historian 26. Answer the 'Analyzing the Evidence' section:

1)

2)

3)

4)

Lone Wolf v. Hichcock

Dawes Severalty Act

Sitting Bull

George A. Custer

Battle of Little Big Horn

Geronimo

Pic 533: What was the photographer-author's *purpose* in removing 'modern' equipment from this?	Map 534: Describe what happened to the size of the Sioux reservations in South Dakota over these 20 years:

Ghost Dance movement

Wounded Knee

Fredrick Jackson Turner

Frontier Thesis

Ohiyesa

Do you agree with Turner that Americans 'need' a frontier, and that with its closing, our pioneering spirit is dwindled and turned inward? If you desire to explore and go beyond, where would you do it? Cyberspace? Outer space?

Pg. 555 17 – INDUSTRIAL AMERICA Tycoon_____
"Hey what's up? We're the .00000001 percent!"

Homestead lockout _____

Pic 545: What happened at the Marianna Mine Disaster? | Could your ancestors have been
                                                      | or known anyone who was at this
                                                      | mine or any other mine at this time?
                                                      |
                                                      |
                                                      |

The 'Gospel of Wealth' _____

Management revolution _____

Andrew Carnegie _____

Pic 546: Describe the general trend in prices between the following years:

1869 to 1890   *1890-1900*   *1869 to 1900*

Pic 547: What did Gustavus Swift do to make the meatpacking industry more efficient?

Vertical integration _____

John D. Rockefeller _____

Horizontal integration _____

Trust _____

J.P. Morgan _____

'Robber barons' _____

'Industrial statesmen' _____

How did shopping change with the rise of Woolworth's, Macy's, Montgomery Ward's and Sears?

Consumer culture

'Blue collar' _____

'White collar' _____

| Pic 549: Along with inventing the electric light bulb, the mimeograph and the movie camera, Thomas Edison, one of the greatest inventors of all time, up there with Archimedes and Leonardo da Vinci, developed the item shown in this picture that would eventually allow recorded sound to be played back: | Pic 550: Do you know any professional salesmen? What do they do at work?

 If you worked in sales, what would you *want* to sell? |

Pic 551: One of the major industries that employed women was _____

Alexander Graham Bell _____

Deskilling _____

Mass production _____

Scientific management _____

| Pic 552: What kinds of manly virtues does this ironworkers painting convey? | Pic 553: How does the Singer company represent an early hint of globalization? |

Thinking Like a Historian 554. Answer the 'Analyzing the Evidence' section:

1)

2)

| Pic 556: Are you offended by the idea of child labor? If so, is *school* a form of child labor- and unpaid at that? Or not? | Map 557: Compare and contrast how the Old and New South were similar and different:

 Similar   *Different* |

Pic 558: Today there are 4,700,000 Mexicans or people of Mexican ancestry living in Los Angeles County. The increase since 1930 has been *Greater Less The Same* as that from between 1900 and 1930.	The three primary growth areas in Europe between these two maps do not include: *Russia Austria-Hungary* *Italy Britain*

America Compared 560. Answer the Questions for Analysis below:

1)

2)

Chinese Exclusion Act

Pics 561 and 564: Why do you think the U.S. practice selective immigration in the past, favoring Europeans and excluding others, such as countrymen of the Chinese workers shown here?

American Voices 562. Answer the Questions for Analysis below:

1)

2)

3)

San Francisco Earthquake

Great Railroad Strike

Henry George

Greenback labor

Producerism

Granger laws

Knights of Labor

Pic 566: Before oil, what was the area around Houston, TX known for?

Pic 567: In the K of L pic here, who is the guy up on the wall and why was he considered a hero?

Anarchism

Haymarket Square

Farmers' Alliance

Hatch Act

Interstate Commerce Clause

Pic 568: What was the *motivation* for this example of industrial violence?

Today, the Interstate Commerce Clause is controversial because in many instances, when a state government has differed in opinions about a topic from the federal government, the federal government has brought them to heel by threatening them with not letting them trade with other states. Do you think that is a form of bullying by the federal government, or do you think central planners and regulators in Washington should keep a tight leash on the state governments?

Closed shop

American Federation of Labor

Leonora Berry

Samuel Gompers

Pg. 574   18 – THE VICTORIANS MAKE THE MODERN   Optimist_____

No more fooling around- its time to make things materially better

Pic 575: Why, in the age of progress and modernity, do you think there were so many 'expositions' and 'world's fairs' held around the world that showcases new things?

_____

Middle class _____

Working class _____

P.T. Barnum _____

Pullman car _____

Pic 576: This train car from over a century ago seems   *nicer*   *less comfortable*   than riding in a modern bus or flying in a modern plane.

Plessy v. Ferguson _____

Thinking Like a Historian 578. Answer the 'Analyzing the Evidence' section:

1)

2)

3)

_____

YMCA _____

What did Teddy Roosevelt think about sports and why?	Pic 580: What kind of values did Horatio Alger promote?

Baseball _____

Negro Leagues _____

[American] Football _____

John Muir

Sierra Club

National Park Service

National Audubon Society

Map 584: Note the names of the national parks and forests in the following states

Maine: *Virginia:*

Kentucky: *Florida:*

Tennessee: *Michigan:*

Arkansas: *Texas:*

Minnesota: *New Mexico:*

North Dakota: *Arizona:*

South Dakota: *Colorado:*

Montana: *Wyoming:*

Idaho: *Utah:*

Oregon: *Washington:*

Nevada: *Hawaii:*

California:

Alaska:

Pic 585: How is Mrs. I.N. Phelps Stokes a 'new woman' in this painting?

Comstock Act

Why was education increasing in its importance in this era?	Pic 586: How is this middle class family different than midcentury families?

Liberal arts

Atlanta Compromise _____

Were there more male or female high school grads in 1910? _____

Maternalism _____

WCTU _____

| Pic 588: What did Booker T. Washington believe about race relations? | Pic 589: Why didn't these intelligent women go to Harvard instead of Radcliffe? |

Pic 590: Who would be most likely to favor a ban on alcohol?

a. German immigrant   b. Irish Bostonian   c. Rural woman in the WCTU

UDC _____

National Association of Colored Women _____

Ida Wells _____

NAWSA _____

NAOWS _____

Feminism _____

What does the term 'heterodox' mean in the context of this era in history?

_____

| Map 593: The present-day states that awarded women the right to vote first were located in: | The present-day states that awarded women the right to vote last were located in: |
| a. the South   b. the Rockies   c. the Northeast | a. the South   b. the Rockies   c. the Northeast |

Darwinism _____

Natural selection _____

Herbert Spencer _____

Social darwinism _____

William Graham Sumner _____

Eugenics

Proponents of eugenics (good genes) believed they could make society better by taking control of the process of human reproduction, like farmers do with plants and animals, and develop better 'strains' of people over time. The opposite, dysgenics, was outlined in degeneration theory. How did they propose to accomplish the eugenic future to make America a 'better place'?

Realism

Naturalism

Name three books by Mark Twain:

1)   2)   3)

Out of the three, circle the number before the one you would choose to read first if you had to.

Modernism

Pic 595: What kinds of topics did the Ash Can school of artists tackle in their works?

American Voices 596. Answer the Questions for Analysis below:

1)

2)

Jack London

Pic 598: If painting dancers in a regular way would have been classified as 'realist', is this painting 'realist' or is it something else?

Pic 599: What are the Protestant American doing in this picture in Japan?

Summarize how the religious landscape of America changed for the following groups:

    Catholic Christians   *Jews*

APA

The Social Gospel

Salvation Army

America Compared 601. Answer the Questions for Analysis below:

1)

2)

3)

'Niagara Creed'

Fundamentalism

Pic 602: What did Billy Sunday preach and what effect did he himself have on the message?

Pg. 606   19 – "CIVILIZATION'S INFERNO"   **Slumlord**_____

Sip an espresso at a café in the Art Deco district and talk about a Monet painting while Debussy is playing in the background, and you'll have "arrived."

Pic 607: What school of art is this picture of a city painted in? | Evaluate whether the Frederic C. Howe quote on pg. 606 is more or less true today than a century ago:
_____ | _____

What effect did the following have on urban patterns?

    Electricity   *Trolley car*   *Els and subways*

What was the 'paradise on earth' that entrepreneur Henry Huntington found?
_____

Chicago school _____

Pic 609: Before the rise of the Empire State Building, this dominated NYC's skyline _____

Pic 610: Do you 'notice' electrical lines and phone lines when you are outside, or do they just fade into the background of the scenery because you are so used to seeing them?
_____

American Voices 611. Answer the Questions for Analysis below:

1)

2)

_____

Pic 612: What is the name of the fault line that caused this? _____

Mutual aid society _____

Pic 613: Name some countries Jews immigrated to America from, based on this map-key: | Why do you thing Jews segregated themselves from each other based on their country of origin?

Race riot

| Pic 614: Who were these middle class blacks in Chicago 'uncomfortable' with? | Pic 615: After a local newspaper reported on four rapes of whites by blacks, the 1906 race riot in this city began: |

Tenements

Vaudeville

Map 616: Note three *influences* on the way Chicago grew and developed in the late-19th century:

1)   2)   3)

What were some of the positives and negatives about the 'dumbell' tenement?

Positives:

Negatives:

Tin Pan Alley

Ragtime

Scott Joplin

Match the amusement park with the city in which it is located:

Amusement Park	*Chicago*
Coney Island	*Long Beach*
Navy Pier	*New York City*

Blues

'Gold digger'

'Queer'

Yellow journalism

Muckrakers

Political machine

Thinking Like a Historian 621. Answer the 'Analyzing the Evidence' section:

1)

2)

3)

Tammany Hall

Boss Tweed

Pic 623: How would *you* advise the city fathers of turn-of-the-century American urban areas to get rid of garbage (remember there are no garbage trucks) like Jacob Riis wants them to?

Tom Johnson

National Municipal League

Progressivism

Pic 625: How do cities invite 'the cholera', according to the cartoon here?	Pic 626: What is 'white slavery' and how was it combatted?

The 'City Beautiful'

Red light district

Social settlement

Hull House

Pic 628: Would you move to a place like Hull House?

   Back then   Today

Jane Addams _____

Margaret Sanger _____

'Birth control' _____

The Jungle _____

Upton Sinclair _____

Pic 629: What did The Jungle advocate the workers in meatpacking facilities do?

_____

Is there any cause you would choose to investigate because you feel it is unjust? What is it?

_____

Pure Food and Drug Act _____

National Consumers' League _____

Women's Trade Union League _____

Triangle Shirtwaist _____

Florence Kelley _____

American Voices 632. Answer the Questions for Analysis below:

1)

2)

3)

_____

Timeline 635: What was Jacob Riis book entitled?

_____

Pg. 636   20 – WHOSE GOVERNMENT?   Idealist_____

Imagine if there was a Ferris wheel so big that you could see back in time & look over the flow of ages past as it becomes our own age.

Pic 637: What trend to encourage political action did Jacob Coxey start in this photograph?

'Waving the bloody shirt'

Gilded Age

What did the term 'Gilded Age' signify in the following spheres:

   Political meaning:

   Economic meaning:

Pendleton Act

Map 639: Relate the voting patterns you see across these three maps of 1880s elections:

Mugwumps

Bureau of Labor Statistics

Thinking Like a Historian 640. Answer the 'Analyzing the Evidence' section:

1)

2)

Sherman Antitrust Act

Lodge Bill

Pic 642: This cartoon expressed the disillusionment of   *Republicans*   *Democrats*

Pic 643: How is this picture similar to people waiting in line at a Trump rally in 2015 and 2016?

Map 643: The populists favored the following political positions and ideas:	The states that voted over 50% for populists were:

What was Coxey's actual proposal for which he rode to Washington at the head of his 'army?'

Free silver

Williams v. Mississippi

Solid South

White Man's Party

William Jennings Bryan

Map 646: How were the state constitutions amended in the years listed in the pink states?	Pic 647: Imprisoned for the murder of a white woman, this black teenager was lynched by a shirt and tie wearing white mob. Why do you think they did they not feel shy about being photographed with the body?

Pic 648: What were W.J. Bryan's political positions?	Go back to pg. 643. How did Bryan's plan contrast with the Omaha Plan?

Map 648: Rate the top 9 states in terms of electoral voting power in the 1896 election:

1   4   7

2   5   8

3   6   9

Pic 649: What did the Supreme Court decide in the following cases:

Lochner v. New York   In re Jacobs   U.S. v. Knight Co.

_____

William McKinley _____

Leon Czolgosz _____

Theodore Roosevelt _____

Elkins Act _____

Square Deal _____

Pic 651: What did TR accomplish in the *Standard Oil* decision?

_____

Monopoly _____

Newlands Reclamation Act _____

Wisconsin Idea _____

Robert La Follette _____

Recall _____

Referendum _____

National Child Labor Com. _____

Muller v. Oregon _____

Louis Brandeis _____

America Compared 653. Answer the Questions for Analysis below:

1)

2)

_____

Pic 654: La Follette's famous quote on reform was: | Pic 655: W.E.B. DuBois' famous book is:

Talented tenth

The Springfield Riot of 1908 began after a series of events beginning with black man breaking into a white family's home. He was chased out by the father, but killed the father in a scuffle down the street. When police caught up with him and another black who was accused of rape, a white mob formed and demanded the police hand them over for [probably] hanging. Instead, the police snuck them out of town for their own safety, and when the mob found out, they rioted in the black neighborhood of the town, shattering the windows of black and Jewish-owned businesses.

What was the group formed by Mary Ovington	What was its goal?	Who became editor of its paper?

NAACP

IWW

New Nationalism

Progressive Party

Why did the election of 1912 feature *four* parties and candidates?

Party 1:   *Platform:*

Candidate:

Party 2:   *Platform:*

Candidate:

Party 3:   *Platform:*

Candidate:

Party 4:   *Platform:*

Candidate:

Pic 656: What does 'class warfare' mean in this context? | Pic 657: What does the elephant symbolize in this image?

American Voices 658. Answer the Questions for Analysis below:

1)

2)

3)

Woodrow Wilson

Eugene V. Debs

William Howard Taft

Map 660: Why didn't Debs get any electoral votes despite winning nearly a million popular votes?

Describe the tax reforms promoted in 1913:

Federal Reserve Act

Wilson signed the controversial Federal Reserve Act after it was shoved through Congress when most of the representatives were home for Christmas. How was the Federal Reserve supposed to work?

Clayton Antitrust Act

Birth of a Nation

Pg. 672 **21 – AN EMERGING WORLD POWER** **Doughboy**_____

Don't worry, he'll keep us out of war. Wink, wink.

Why do you think it made political sense for Wilson to add Bryan to his Cabinet?
_____

American exceptionalism

How did the following influence Americans who believed in the exceptionality of their country?

Our Country   *Social Darwinism*   *Influence of Sea Power upon History*

William Randolph Hurst

'Remember the Maine'

Teller Amendment

George Dewey

Why did the U.S. go to war against Spain- and what led to U.S. victory?

   Causes   *Reasons for outcome*

Rough Riders

Pic 676: Why was the last queen of Hawaii imprisoned?	Pic 677: What happened at the Battle of San Juan Hill?

Philippines

Do you think the U.S. should be considered an 'empire' in this era, when the Philippines was a colony of America?

Insular Cases

Platt Amendment

Emilio Aguinaldo

'Open door'

Pic 697: Which country acted as an independent buffer zone between French Indochina and British Burma?	Which power had influence over the Yangtze River in China?

American Voices 680. Answer the Questions for Analysis below:

1)

2)

3)

Root-Takahira Agreement

What did TR mean by 'big stick' in his famous quote? _____

Panama Canal

Roosevelt Corollary

Pic 682: Note three dangers Panama Canal workers faced when digging the canal:	Map 683: Note the places the U.S. intervened
1	1 5
2	2 6
3	3 7
	4 8 9

Pic 684: How did the Mexican Revolution affect the U.S. and what was Porfirio Diaz' role?

Pancho Villa

Triple Alliance _____

Triple Entente _____

Franz Ferdinand _____

Hiram Maxim _____

Machine Gun _____

Neutrality _____

Pic 685: What was Eddie Rickenbacker's role in WWI? _____

Unterseeboot _____

Lusitania _____

Zimmerman Telegram _____

What evidence of 'Wilsonian idealism' resides in the quotes from Wilson on pg. 686?	Pic 687: What did the film shown have to do with WWI?

Bolsheviks _____

Vladimir Lenin _____

'Doughboys' _____

Map 688: Draw the front line below, and label the five major battles U.S. soldiers participated in:

Influenza Pandemic _____

War Industries Board _____

National War Labor Board

America Compared 689. Answer the Questions for Analysis below:

1)

2)

Pic 690: The Flu of 1918-19 was the worst in history in terms of deaths. Note the following:

How it began and diffused   *How it was fought*

Committee on Public Information

Four-Minute Men

Sedition Act

Pics 691: In WWI and WWII propaganda posters were made in all belligerent countries. They promoted the goals of the respective governments or other organizations, such as the Red Cross. Sometimes they contained outright propaganda, depicting the enemy, whether German, French, Japanese, Russian or American, as something lower than human and not worthy of one's higher morality. Other times they were pleas for help, and sometimes they idealized the cause, or asked for public help in financing the war. Both these images are asking people to buy war bonds, which means spending money by buying a piece of paper that will gain value once you trade it in after the war, in exchange for your money today. However, the *reasons* for buying the bonds are different in these images. How so? What are they appealing to?

Note the results of the following cases:

Schenck v. United States   *Abrams v. United States*

Thinking Like a Historian 692. Answer the 'Analyzing the Evidence' section:

1)

2)

3)

Pic 694: The barrenness of the landscape in this image is symbolic of   a. hope   b. desperation

Great Migration

Pic 695: What kinds of jobs did women take during the war to help fill the labor shortage?

NWP

Alice Paul

Versailles Conference

Fourteen Points

League of Nations

Pic 696: What methods does this image use to try and gain equal pay for equal work for women?	Pic 697: Why do you think the caption calls this cartoon 'scathing'?

David Lloyd George

Georges Clemenceau

Reparations

Self-determination

Arthur Balfour met with Lord Rothschild, a leader of the Jewish community, and together they devised the Balfour Declaration stating Britain's support for a Jewish state in Palestine after the war. Why was Britain in a unique position to influence the opening of this region to Jewish migration?

Map 698: List the following border changes after WWI:

New and Reconstituted Nations   *Allied Occupation*   *British Mandates*   *French Mandates*

Henry Cabot Lodge

Article X

If you were a lawyer arguing both sides of the following case, what would your main points be?

The U.S. should join the League of Nations   *The U.S. should not join the League of Nations*

If you were a lawyer arguing both sides of the following case, what would your main points be?

Wilson was right when he said the war was being fought to 'make the world safe for democracy'   *The war was not fought for that reason*

Pg. 704 22 – CULTURAL CONFLICT, BUBBLE AND BUST Flapper_____

Hey, psst? What's the secret code to get into the Great Gatsby party?

Why did some Americans feel that actors like Valentino made bad role models?	What was Wilbur Crafts' accusation of Hollywood? Why did he think the movie industry was not in 'American' control'?

Pic 705: Note some of the slang terms on the flags from the 1920s:

_____

Pic 706: What were some of the causes of the following race riots of the post-WWI period?

    Chicago   *East St. Louis*   *Tulsa*

_____

Was future president Calvin Coolidge pro or anti-organized labor? _____

How did the courts rule in the following cases involving organized labor:

Coronado Coal v. United Mine Workers	*Adkins v. Children's Hospital*	*Muller v. Oregon*

Pic 707: What do the following terms mean in the context of this period of time?

    Bolshevism   *Red Scare*

_____

Welfare capitalism

Henry Ford

Palmer raids

Pic 708: What about the Sacco and Vanzetti case is noteworthy?

Sheppard-Towner Act

ERA

WILPF

Warren G. Harding

Associated state

Teapot Dome

Dollar diplomacy

Prohibition

ACLU

Scopes Trial

What form of American nativism took hold in the early-1920s related to immigration levels?

National Origins Act

Pic 714: After the 1924 act, the U.S. established _____ to guard the Mexican border.

KKK

What evidence did Henry Ford have for his claim that America was caught up in an international Jewish world conspiracy?

Herbert Hoover

Hoover hostesses

Map 715: Did any states have the trifecta of Klan violence, Klan support for the governor *and* Klan support for a senator? | Are there any places that surprise you for not having much Klan activity in this period?

Thinking Like a Historian 716. Answer the 'Analyzing the Evidence' section:

1)

2)

3)

4)

Harlem Renaissance

Zora Neale Hurston

Franz Boas

Jazz

Louis Armstrong

Pic 718: Are there any hints of leftover sectional differences from the Civil War-era on this map?

'Slumming'

UNIA

Why did Marcus Garvey- a black leader- argue for segregation and racial separation?

Pan-Africanism

Pics 720: Discuss the aspects of the black experience of the Interwar era shown in these images:

Lost Generation

Note the messages of the following books of the age:

The Three Soldiers *A Farewell to Arms* *Desire Under the Elms*

The Emperor Jones *Babbitt* *Elmer Gantry*

The Great Gatsby

'Roaring '20s'

United Fruit Company

Wall Street

American Voices 723. Answer the Questions for Analysis below:

1)

2)

3)

Self-Help

Consumer credit

Pic 724: Recently, commercials for bananas on TV called it, "Quite possibly the world's perfect food." How is this image similar to a modern TV commercial?

Automobiles

Pic 725: What did the rise of the automobile do for many people in the middle class?

Hollywood _____

Flapper _____

Adolf Zucker _____

'American Dream' _____

Soft power _____

Place an appropriate check next to the major films of the 1930s:

	Seen it!	Heard of it	Never heard			Seen it!	Heard of it	Never heard
Our Daily Bread	___	___	___		Steamboat Willie	___	___	___
Grapes of Wrath	___	___	___		Snow White	___	___	___
Mr. Deeds Goes to Town	___	___	___		Wizard of Oz	___	___	___
Mr. Deeds... Washington	___	___	___		Gone with the Wind	___	___	___
Meet John Doe	___	___	___		It's a Wonderful Life	___	___	___
Little Caesar	___	___	___		Why We Fight	___	___	___
The Public Enemy	___	___	___					
Gold Diggers	___	___	___		Heard of any other movies from the '30s?			
It Happened One Night	___	___	___					

America Compared 14. Answer the Questions for Analysis below:

1)

2)

_____

Pic 726: Have you ever seen Charlie Chaplin acting on a screen before? _____

Buying 'on the margin' _____

Graph 728: The height of the Great Depression, when the unemployment rate was highest, was in the year	Pic 729: Why did farmers, poor as they were, have a one-up on city folk in the Depression?

Pg. 734   **23 – MANAGING THE GREAT DEPRESSION**   **Tariff slapper_____**

If you have gum in school, even if you shouldn't, go ahead and blow a bubble till it pops and say, "That was this whole chapter in miniature."

What was the 'new form of liberalism' represented by the New Deal? | Pic 735: Rate the following in importance when YOU look for a job (1-4)

| Pay   Working Conditions

| Meals   Surroundings

Smoot-Hawley Tariff

America Compared 737. Answer the Questions for Analysis below:

1)

2)

'Hoovervilles'

'Hoover blankets'

Bonus Army

Pic 738: If you lost your home, would you consider building a shack and living in a Hooverville? | Map 739: Circle the state you'd probably rather be living in during the Depression

| a. Georgia   b. Maine   c. Michigan

Fireside chats

Hundred Days

Glass-Steagall Act

Note what the following agencies were and what they did:

FDIC   AAA   NRA   FERA   PWA   CWA   CCC

Table 741: The worst year for bank lolfails was _____

American Voices 743. Answer the Questions for Analysis below:

1)

2)

3)

FHA _____

Pic 745: How many CCC units did your state have during the New Deal? _____

SEC _____

Liberty League _____

NAM _____

Schechter v. U.S. _____

Townsend Plan _____

Huey Long _____

Charles Coughlin _____

Pic 746: Father Coughlin believed, like Henry Ford and Charles Lindbergh, in the anti-Semitic theory that the Depression was being engineered to some extent by Jewish bankers speculating and setting monetary policy on the economies in the U.S. and Europe. What did Coughlin argue FDR should do?

Welfare state _____

NLRB _____

Social Security Act _____

ADC/AFDC _____

Pic 749: Where did this sit-down strike take place? _____

Contrast classical liberalism vs. New Deal liberalism:

Classical liberalism   *New Deal liberalism*

Map 748: Note the major popular protests of the 1930s by year:

1930-31   *1932-33*   *1934-35*   *1936-37*   *1938-39*

WPA

When the authors state FDR's Supreme Court appointees were chosen in part because they all believed the Constitution was a 'living document', what do they mean?

Roosevelt recession

Keynesian economics

Thinking Like a Historian 752. Answer the 'Analyzing the Evidence' section:

1)

2)

3)

Frances Perkins

Pic 754: What does it mean to say the Roosevelts were a 'patrician family'?

Mary McLeod Methune

Eleanor Roosevelt

Resettlement Administration

'Black Cabinet'

Pic 756: How did the Scottsboro case impact the American judicial system?

John Collier

Indian Reorganization Act

Pic 757: Note some reasons *not* all tribes welcomed the New Deal's Indian policies:	Pic 758: What are the Mexicans- both American and immigrant- asking for from the government?

Dust Bowl

'Okies'

The Grapes of Wrath

Map 759: What five states were impacted in part by the severe wind erosion in the Dust Bowl?	Pic 760: This picture is in every U.S. history textbook. Seriously. If you are in your class right now, ask your teacher to see another U.S. history text from the shelf and check it. Was it there? Y N Now ask why.

TVA

REA

Hoover Dam

Grand Coulee

Pg. 766 — 24 – THE WORLD AT WAR — Riveter _____
It's go time.

WWII became known as the 'good war'. For what two reasons did the government justify U.S. involvement, one during and one after the war?

During: *After:*

Fascism _____

List the fascist rulers of the following countries:

Italy: *Germany:*   *Japan:*

Hitler promoted the doctrine of Aryan racial supremacy. What did that mean?

_____

Il Duce _____

Nazi Party _____

Reichstag _____

__Mein Kampf__ _____

__Lebensraum__ _____

Rome-Berlin Axis _____

Gerald Nye _____

Neutrality Act _____

Pic 769: Describe the atmosphere at the Nuremberg rallies in one word:	Pic 770: The standoff here is between Lindbergh, who wanted: _____ And 'Democracy', who wanted: _____
_____	

Popular Front _____

Munich Conference _____

Nonaggression Pact _____

Interventionists were known as internationalists. What did they want America to do?

_____

FDR, who broke the Neutrality Act by making a deal with Britain and said, "America must be the great arsenal of democracy," is best classified as:

a. an isolationist   b. an interventionist

What were Roosevelt's 'Four Freedoms'?

1	2	Of them, do you see any as most important?
3	4	

America First Committee

Lend-Lease Act

Atlantic Charter

'Rape of Nanjing'

Greater East Asia Co-Prosperity Sphere

Pearl Harbor

War Powers Act

Pic 772: What do you think the term one city (and island) at a time means in the context of WWII?

Graph 773: When was the only time that U.S. defense spending was more than regular spending? Copy the chart:

30

20

10
5
0
      1930   1940   1950   1960   1970   1980

America Compared 14. Answer the Questions for Analysis below:

1)

2)

3)

Revenue Act

Pic 775: What are these workers doing?	How did the war affect the relationship betwixt large corporations like Ford and GM and the government?

Code talkers

WAC

WAVES

'Rosie the Riveter'

Pic 777: How was the traditional woman's role of protector and nurturer of the family incorporated into Rosie's job description?

American Voices 778. Answer the Questions for Analysis below:

1)

2)

3)

Executive Order 8802

Pic 780: What are these protest signs asking for?

Bracero Program

Smith-Connelly Labor Act

Servicemen's Readjustment Act

OWI

Why We Fight

| What is rationing, and what kind of items were rationed in American during WWII? | The Detroit Riot of 1943 started on Belle Isle, an island park in the Detroit River. A year earlier, the government built a black housing project in the middle of the Polish white neighborhood, which stirred tensions. How many died in this riot? |

Zoot suits

Thinking Like a Historian 784. Answer the 'Analyzing the Evidence' section:

1)

2)

3)

Pic 786 (top): The Zoot suit riots began a few days after a U.S. Navy enlisted man's jaw was broken by zoot suit wearing street fighters in LA, while the sailor's friends were on the other side of the street talking to girls. Why are these riots seen as having shown 'cracks in wartime unity'?

Pic 786 (bot.): Pete Seeger was around a long time. Youtube: *Garden Song Pete Seeger* to hear him at his folksy best. But he was a supporter of Soviet Communism as well. What is he advocating for here?

Executive Order 9066

"A Jap is a Jap, whether he is an American citizen or not," said John DeWitt. Now say you moved to China permanently, then the United States began bombing China and China declared war on the U.S. In the case, would you be pro-China defeating the U.S., or pro-American because that's what you 'are,' even though you moved to China?

Map 787: What part of the country were Japanese-descended people banned from?

Pic 788: Selected suspension of citizen rights is something that happens in some wars, in some countries, depending on law, and what that country's leadership thinks is prudent during wartime. The latest research shows 36,000 noncitizen Japanese (enemy aliens) were interned, as well as 14,000 Germans and Italians. To this number, however, were added 71,000 Japanese-Americans (citizens) who were brought to relocation centers, in a suspension of *habeas corpus*. Was this necessary in your opinion for either of the groups? When, if ever, should regular legal processes be set-aside during wartime for the following:

"ENEMY ALIENS"	CITIZENS OF "ENEMY" DESCENT

Korematsu v. U.S.

The Soviet Union was fighting a 'deep war' with Germany. Probably the deepest deep war that was ever fought. How many did they lose at the Battle of Kursk?

Pic 789: What was the objective of the soldiers pictured here?

Battle of Stalingrad

'Turn of the tide'

Map 790-791: Note the major battles that took place in the following locations, but place the battles on the right-hand map from the later part of the war underneath those from the left map.

North Africa *Soviet Union* *Italy* *France* *Germany*

D-Day

How many German civilians were killed by Allied bombing raids on Hamburg and Dresden?	Note the significance of the Battle of the Bulge:

Jewish emigration from Germany was encouraged via the Haavara Transfer Agreement (1933), whereby Jews deposited money into an account in Germany where it was used to buy tools and equipment needed to build a new Jewish state in Palestine, migrated to Palestine, then got the money back from a bank in Tel-Aviv run by a Jewish company after the tools had been sold to previous settlers. Ten percent of Germany's Jews migrated under the Transfer Agreement, to the point where Tel Aviv came to be the world's foremost example of a Bauhaus city, built in a modernist architectural style brought from Europe by the new arrivals. But many Jews did not migrate, until the fateful voyage of the *St. Louis.* What happened to it?

Holocaust

Henry Morgenthau

Battle of Leyte Gulf

How did the Americans treat the Japanese as inferior people compared to them?	How did the Japanese treat others with their own sense of racial superiority?

Manhattan Project

J. Robert Oppenheimer

Maps 793-794: Using both maps, place the battles in chronological order:

Year	Battle	Year	Battle
1941	Pearl Harbor		

Pic 795: Who were the 'Big 3' and what did they accomplish (or give up) at Yalta?

Pic 796: Would you have dropped the bomb like Truman did? _____

Pg. 804   **25 – COLD WAR AMERICA**   **Spy**_____

Better dead than red. Till you realize most of them actually hate their government just like we do. Then you just feel sorry for everyone.

In the battle of ideologies, authoritarian communist vs. liberal democratic, both sides painted the other as objectively bad. In the Soviet Union, peasants were told their crops were not growing well because the Americans were dropping poison out of high-flying airplanes at night. In the U.S., the hunt was on for 'subversives', people trying to undermine American society. Do you think people should always be on the lookout for those who may do harm to society? Or is that too oppressive sounding?

___

Yalta Conference

UN

Potsdam Conference

Iron Curtain

How did American and Soviet viewpoints differ about the postwar world order?

___

Pic 806: Did this friendliness last? | Map 808: At right, sketch the inset map of Berlin and label the zones:

Containment

George F. Kennan

Truman Doctrine

Thinking Like a Historian 26. Answer the 'Analyzing the Evidence' section:

1)

2)

3)

Marshall Plan

NATO

Warsaw Pact

COMECON

NSC-68

| Pic 812: Why didn't some war torn countries like Poland, Czechoslovakia, and Hungary accept Marshall Plan aid when even former U.S. adversaries like West Germany and Japan did? | Pic 813: The Berlin Airlift

a. was a Western victory

b. helped spur on Cold War tension

c. both of these |

America Compared 814. Answer the Questions for Analysis below:

1)

2)

Robert Taft

| Pic 815 (top): What evidence do you see here of propaganda imagery? | Pic 815 (bot.): Note the 'first' for the American military that the Korean War was the scene of: |

Map 816: Summarize the major stages of the 'forgotten war':

1)

2)

3)

4)

5)

38th Parallel

Why did President Truman relieve General MacArthur of command- and do you think it was right?

Map 817: What do you think Eisenhower meant when he used the label "military-industrial complex" in his farewell speech to the country, which is available on Youtube?	Name 5 military-industrial companies:

Graph 818: About what year, if any, did American total spending surpass the amount spent at the peak of WWII?	About what year did defense spending surpass WWII levels?

Cold War liberalism

Taft-Hartley Act

Pic 819: Who were the main candidates in the 1948 election and why is this sign in the picture so famous?

Candidates: *Sign:*

Fair Deal

In 1951, Julius and Ethyl Rosenberg were arrested for treason and found guilty of giving nuclear secrets to Soviet agents. They were executed. If you suspected your neighbor had terrorist ties, would you report that, or would you remain quiet? Evaluate:

Reasons I might not report them   *Reasons I might report them*

Loyalty-Security Program

HUAC

McCarthyism

American Voices 822. Answer the Questions for Analysis below:

1)

2)

3)

___

Pic 824: What is on the board that McCarthy is using as his main visual exhibit here?

___

Dwight Eisenhower

Nikita Khrushchev

'New Look'

John Foster Dulles

Third World

Domino theory

Ho Chi Minh

Zionism

Israel

Gemal Abdel Nasser

Eisenhower Doctrine

Pic 829: What is the 'Suez', and why did the Suez Crisis break out?

___

John F. Kennedy

New Frontier

Bay of Pigs

Fidel Castro

Map 831: Which island contained the most U.S. bases in the Caribbean? _____

Cuban Missile Crisis

The Soviets demanded, in exchange for removal of the missiles from Cuba, that the U.S. remove missiles from Turkey, which was across the Black Sea from the USSR. Do you think it was a fair deal to deescalate the situation, or should the U.S. have held firm and demanded the Soviets remove their missiles without promising to remove American missiles from the Soviet sphere?

Peace Corps

The Peace Corps Kennedy began has come under fire recently after being accused of covering up the fact that over 1,000 female Peace Corps volunteers have been sexually attacked by people in countries in Africa, the Middle East and Asia that they are trying to help out in, in the past decade. In Kennedy's time, if that happened the American would have had the full weight of the nation behind them. Today, not so much. Their cases get lost in bureaucracy. A volunteer named Nick Castle was murdered in China a few years ago, and- did anyone know? Other lurid stories are told. Do you think as a government agency, the Peace Corp should reveal all this to volunteers *before* they sign up, or let them be transferred to a country that may be dangerous without telling them?

Pic 832: Was the Berlin Wall pictured here built to keep people out, or to keep people in? Why?

Brinksmanship

There is an anomaly in your textbook. In a book all about American history, they forgot to put a page or two about Americans who landed on the Moon. Actually, they left out space altogether. Why? I don't know. But maybe they don't want you to be proud that we were able to do it. Think about it: Louis Armstrong, a trumpeter, is in the book, but Neil Armstrong, the first human being to walk on another celestial body, is totally erased from your advanced high school history course. See the problem? Look in the index and try to find him or Buzz Aldrin, or Michael Collins, who orbited while they were on the Moon and picked them up. The NASA mission's name was Project Apollo, and adjusted for inflation, the entire program, including all the research and development of products and equipment, all the training, and the six landings, cost 109 billion dollars. A mission to Mars program is estimated by NASA to cost about the same over ten years' time. The wars in the Middle East since Sept. 11th, on the other hand, have cost 1,700 billion dollars, as of 2015. If America didn't have to deal with that or chose not to, about how many times could we have already established a human presence on Mars? Do you think that would have been a better option? Why or why not?

Pg. 838   26 – TRIUMPH OF THE MIDDLE CLASS   Consumer_____

"Roger that Houston, the Affluent Society has landed."

Pic 839: The 'middle class family' has become something of cliché in America. People make fun of happy families that have a medium-sized house in a nice neighborhood, and barbeque on weekends. They make fun of families that have both a mom and a dad, say the people who emerge from such environments are privileged and should have nothing to be proud of because everyone labored for them in some way, even if indirectly, to support their 'consumer culture.' Nothing they can do is right. Just read the last paragraph on pg. 838. Do you agree with this assessment of the family shown, or is there more to the middle class than meets the eye?

_____

Bretton Woods _____

World Bank _____

IMF _____

Pic 840: In the kitchen debate, who 'won'? (as in, which country boasted better consumer products, the USA or the USSR?)

Pic 841: Why would a company like Boeing be glad of the government ordered new equipment from them?

Sputnik _____

National Defense Education Act _____

UAW _____

The Affluent Society _____

The Other America _____

GI Bill _____

VA _____

Pic 844: Do you think it was a good idea for the government to loan or donate money to former GIs (an acronym for Government Issue, as in the uniforms soldiers get when they report for duty) who want to reintegrate into society after the war is over? Why or why not?

_____

Collective bargaining _____

Planned obsolescence

How did television change the American lifestyle? | Name four important '50s TV shows:

Teenager

Pic 846: Why are these teens so ecstatic and what does that say about how teens came to self-identify in a new way? | Pic 847: How is a Motorola TV meaningful to:
| *Mom:*
| *Dad:*
| *Kids:*
| *Older folks:*

Rock n' Roll

Beat Generation

What did Beats like Jack Kerouac think about politics? | Pic 848: Youtube the Supremes song *Reflections* and you will get a sense of their style at their best. Why did they call the city they were from 'Motown?'

Pic 849: Communism *was* godless, in the sense the government outlawed or persecuted Christianity and shut down churches, and communist governments lowered the value of human life to the point human beings were expendable without a second thought, to the tune of 100,000,000 needlessly dead. But the house the Marx built was opposed by Billy Graham. What was his message?

Companionate marriage

Domesticity

Baby boom

Describe three 'miracle drugs' introduced in this era:

1　　　　　　　　　　2　　　　　　　　　　3

Dr. Spock

American Voices 32. Answer the Questions for Analysis below:

1)

2)

3)

4)

5)

| Pic 854: How come signs in the '50s advertised 'help wanted male' and 'help wanted female' instead of just 'help wanted'? | How did the Supreme Court ruling in Griswold v. Connecticut change dating and marriage patterns? |

Alfred Kinsey

Homophilia

What was Hugh Heffner trying to promote in Playboy Magazine in contradistinction to middle class morality?

Housing boom

Levittown

Shelley v. Kraemer

Little League

Interstate Highways Act

This space intentionally left empty

Thinking Like a Historian 26. Answer the 'Analyzing the Evidence' section:

1)

2)

3)

4)

America Compared 860. Answer the Questions for Analysis below:

1)

2)

3)

Fast food

Shopping mall

Map 861: Most I (interstate) highways are located   a. east   b. west   of the Mississippi River.

Pic 861: Do you think the reason most Americans don't eat healthy food all the time is because it…

a. takes too long to cook   b. is more expensive than fast food   c. both of these

Sunbelt

Walt Disney

Map 862: Note three Sunbelt states that had over 200% growth:

Kerner Commission

How did the government try to solve the 'urban crisis'?

Pg. 868 27 – WALKING INTO FREEDOM LAND Groovy cat_____

Some say liberalism is the ideology of Western suicide. Others say it is our salvation. It can be one or the other, but it can't be both.

Rights liberalism

Pic 869: Here you see the Reverend Dr. Martin Luther King Jr. entering Montgomery, the capital of Alabama. Why did he undertake this march from Selma?

Jim Crow

Pic 870: Note the kinds of public places that were segregated into 'white' and 'colored' only areas:

How did WWII and later the idea of mass democracy help break down the traditional belief that races should remain unmixed, according to Langston Hughes?

Brotherhood of Sleeping Car Porters

Double V

CORE

Pic 872: What led Truman to desegregate the armed forces in 1948?

Pic 873: Like white women, black women got jobs during the war doing things like this, in the picture:

Map 874: The most blacks left the following state _____ and headed for _____

'To secure these rights'

Dixiecrats

Barrio

Many Mexicans of non-Spanish descent leave Mexico to escape what they see as a *casta* race/class hierarchy there. When they came to America, what did they find that disheartened them?

America Compared 876. Answer the Questions for Analysis below:

1)

2)

3)

Pic 877: If you were a border agent inspecting this Bracero worker's ID, determine the following:

What city is he from: *Where was the card issued:*

When was he born: *When was it issued:*

American GI Forum

Brown v. Board of Education

Caesar Chavez

Dolores Huerta

Thurgood Marshall

What did Marshall accomplish for the black community in the following cases:

Smith v. Allwright *McLaurin v. Oklahoma*

'Black Monday'

Little Rock Central High School

Map 879: Summarize the landmark civil rights cases across the country in chronological order:

	Year	Case	Outcome
1			
2			
3			

4

5

6

7

8

9

10

Emmett Till

During the Emmett Till trial, the jury decided by race, and it was called a 'miscarriage of justice.' Do you think people on a jury today could do that? If so, are jury trials out of date in a multicultural society? Explain.

Montgomery Bus Boycott

Rosa Parks

Pic 880 and 881: What would Marcus Garvey, the founder of Pan-Africanism and a black separatist, have said about the events in these pictures?

SCLC

Sit-in

SNCC

Freedom ride

Letter from a Birmingham Jail

Martin Luther King

George Wallace

George Wallace was the last candidate in American history to run on a segregationist platform for president. What were some of the things he spoke out about that gained him so many votes?

American Voices 885. Answer the Questions for Analysis below:

1)

2)

3)

4)

March on Washington

Map 887: Summarize the landmark moments in the civil rights struggle in chronological order:

	Year	Event
1		
2		
3		
4		
5		
6		
7		
8		
9		
10		

Thinking Like a Historian 26. Answer the 'Analyzing the Evidence' section:

1)

2)

3)

Civil Rights Act

MS Freedom Democratic Party

Voting Rights Act

Pic 890: How did women contribute to the civil rights movement?	Map 891: Which state had the fewest blacks enrolled in 1964 compared to in 1975?

Black nationalism

Nation of Islam

Malcolm X

Black Power

Pic 893: Malcolm X, a proponent of black supremacy and the rejection of white society, is wearing a European suit. Is that cultural appropriation by stealth, or should that standard not apply?

Black Panther Party

YLO

Pic 894: What political philosophy did the Black Panthers profess?

Map 895: List the colonies that became independent states in each of the following decades:

1940s

1950s

1960s

1970s

'Long hot summer' _____

Watts Riot _____

Why was President Johnson, who just enacted the Great Society legislation to help poor people, so despondent upon hearing the news from the large cities about rioting?

_____

Did all blacks agree that what they needed was Martin Luther King's 'dream' of a multiracial society? If not, what did they say they wanted?

_____

UFW _____

MAPA _____

MALDF _____

Chicano/Chicana _____

Pic 897: Which type of civil disobedience did both Chavez and King advocate? _____

AIM _____

Alcatraz _____

Pic 898: If you were to try and 'retake' a place in the world that formerly belonged to your ancestors, what would it be and how would you go about doing it?

_____

Pg. 902 — 28 – LIBERALISM AND CONSERVATIVE REBIRTH — Disco dancer _____

What do you want to do today? "Overturn the existing society dude." What do we replace it with? "I don't know, something groovy!"

Pic 903: What does Uncle Sam want out of in this picture?

Great Society

Economic Opportunity Act

Lyndon Johnson

Pic 905: Why do you think LBJ wanted a photo op with this particular family on the campign to promote the Great Society?

Barry Goldwater

Medicare

Medicaid

Secondary Education Act

Higher Education Act

HUD

Table 907: Summarize the seventeen Great Society programs below, and rate them 1-3 as to how important they are to you personally

	Program	Summary	Rating
1			
2			
3			
4			
5			
6			
7			

8

9

10

11

12

13

14

15

16

17

Map 906: Which geographic area of the country voted for Goldwater? _____

Graph 908: Considering the qualifications for being in poverty have shifted over the last 50 years, do you think the War on Poverty was a success? Is it still going on?

Equal Pay Act

Betty Friedan

The Feminine Mystique

Presidential Commission on the Status of Women

NOW

Pic 909: If women's suffrage was the overarching goal of the 'First Wave' feminists of the 1920s, what were the goals of these 'Second Wave' feminists of the 1960s?

Ngo Dinh Diem

Gulf of Tonkin Resolution

Map 910: The Ho Chi Minh Trail wound through these countries:

_____   _____   _____

Operation Rolling Thunder

Graph 911: In which year did U.S. military presence in Vietnam surpass 500,000 people?

    a. 1965   b. 1968   c. 1972   d. 1968 B.C.

American Voices 913. Answer the Questions for Analysis below:

1)

2)

3)

SDS

Port Huron Statement

New Left

Pic 915: During the Free Speech rallies at UC Berkeley, what messages were the protesters trying to convey concerning the following:

    Vietnam War   *Social Issues*   *Free Speech*

YAF

Thinking Like a Historian 917. Answer the 'Analyzing the Evidence' section:

1)

2)

3)

Sharon Statement

Counterculture

Beatlemania

'Flower children'

Pic 918: "Today, the counterculture of the 1960s is the dominant culture, mainstream even, while traditional culture is a kind of counterculture." Do you agree or disagree with this statement?	If you had been alive when Woodstock was going on, would you go to the festival? Why or why not?

Tet Offensive

Robert Kennedy

America Compared 920. Answer the Questions for Analysis below:

1)

2)

Democratic Convention

Yippies

Pic 921: Who assassinated Robert Kennedy and what was his motivation?

Hubert H. Humphrey

Richard Nixon

George Wallace

Pic 922: Youtube: *George Wallace Segregation Now* to hear the last speech by a presidential candidate that advocated race separatism. Aside from segregation, however, what other issues with broader popular appeal nationwide did Wallace touch on?

What states or part of states did Wallace carry in Map 923?

Chicano Moratorium Committee

Pic 924: Muhammad Ali was seem like an unlikely supporter of George Wallace, but Youtube: *Muhammad Ali Race* and watch him defend a segregationist position. Ali converted to Islam and visited Africa, was a world champion boxer and well traveled. Whether you agree with his position on Vietnam or not, do you agree with the decision to strip him of his title?

Title IX

Gloria Steinem

Pic 925: If *Ms.* magazine was still on the market, would you read it? Why or why not?	Pic 926: The process of 'coming out' began on a large scale in the 1960s. What is this process?

Stonewall Inn

Silent majority

Vietnamization

Kent State incident

Pic 927: Certain people didn't like Obama, Bush, the Clintons or others. But there was one president that *everybody* hated: Nixon. But it was not always so, and he might have gotten a worse wrap than he deserves. Youtube: *Nixon Checkers Speech* to see the guy in action and decide for yourself. But one thing is certain- Nixon's comeback was perhaps the greatest in American political history. He lost the 1960 election to Kennedy, then he lost when he ran for governor of California. His career should have been over. But he never let up, and now, at the Apollo 11 landing site in the Sea of Tranquility on the Moon, there is a plaque (Wikipedia: *Lunar Plaque*) that reads, "Here men from the Planet Earth first set foot upon the Moon, July, 1969 A.D. We came in peace for all mankind." The plaque is signed Neil Armstrong, Buzz Aldrin and Michael Collins. And underneath their names, there is another signature, that of President of the United States Richard Nixon. No other president's name is on the Moon. What did the people who loved Nixon in 1968 love him for?

My Lai

Détente

Henry Kissinger

SALT I

Today, presidents are hesitant to visit or entertain leaders from countries whose stated policies are anti-American, such as Iran or North Korea. Presidents have said they would not dream of entertaining such leaders. But in the 1960s, Nixon visited China. Why? And what resulted?

| Pic 930: After America left Vietnam to its own devices, Saigon was renamed. What was the new name and why?

Warren Court

Note the decisions made in the famous trials of the Warren Court:

Brown v. Board of Ed.   *Miranda v. Arizona*   *Roth v. United States*

Miller v. California   *Milliken v. Bradley*

Pic 931: Do you agree or disagree with the anti-busing protesters?

| Map 932: This election:
|
| *a. was close*
|
| *b. was a blow out*

Pg. 936   29 – THE SEARCH FOR ORDER IN AN ERA OF LIMITS   Populist_____

American society was hep in the 40s, swell in the 50s, groovy in the 60s, radical in the 70s, awesome in the 80s, and totally fly in the 90s

Why was the TV show *All in the Family* an effective reflection of American society in the 1970s?

Pic 937: Would you work here if they were hiring?

OPEC

Graph 938: Categorize the following energy sources:

Those which rose dramatically in usage	Those that stagnated or rose moderately

'Gas guzzlers'

Energy crisis

Silent Spring

Environmentalism

Earth Day

Pic 939: Which holiday do you actually celebrate the most:

a. Earth Day   b. Arbor Day   c. Columbus Day   d. Washington's Birthday

Thinking Like a Historian 26. Answer the 'Analyzing the Evidence' section:

1)

2)

3)

Three Mile Island

Stagflation

Inflation

Pic 943: In the late-1970s, Chinese president Deng Xiaoping met with President Carter and hammered out a deal whereby communist China would open up areas of the country to American investment. This helped spur the deindustrialization of the country, as many companies, starting with textiles (shoes, clothes etc.) moved there to take advantage of the plentiful labor supply, lack of a minimum wage, and lax or nonexistent environmental regulations. What did it help do to the industrial landscape of America, and is it time to adjust the policy of free trade, in vogue since the 1970s, to favor investment in the United States again?

Deindustrialization

Rust Belt

Map 944: In which two general directions did American migrate within the country during this era?	Pic 945: When Ford 'said' *drop dead* to the city, what did he 'mean'?

Tax revolt

Prop. 13

Watergate

War Powers Act

Freedom of Info Act

Ethics in Gov Act

Jimmy Carter

Graph 949: Is your state on the list? What happened to the electoral votes in your state?

Pic 950: Does this down home image suit Jimmy Carter's character? Why or why not?

| How successful was Carter in implementing his agenda?

Deregulation

Affirmative Action

Bakke v. California

Pic 951: Do you agree that Affirmative Action, the legal requirement that businesses above a certain size hire a certain percentage of nonwhite males and women, fulfills the ideal of 'equal opportunity'? Or do you agree with his opponents that equal opportunity should be based solely on merit and the decisions arrived at by the business owners themselves? If you were a lawyer arguing both sides of the case, what would your main points be?

Affirmative Action is good for America	*Affirmative Action is not good for America*

Prop 209

ERA

Stop ERA

Roe v. Wade

Pic 952: Why is this woman against what many people saw as empowering to women?

| Map 953: Did your state ratify ERA or not? If so, what year did they do it?
|
| _____
|
| Would you have supported it?

Phyllis Schlafly

American Voices 954. Answer the Questions for Analysis below:

1)

2)

3)

Pic 956: What was significant about Harvey Milk? | What was his fate?

Graph 958: Describe what happened to the following indices between 1970 and 2000:

Husband only earning:

Wife only earning:

Both earning:

No earners:

Pic 959 (top): What do you think the deeper forces were that caused the 'blue-collar blues' in the '70s? | Pic 959 (bot.): How is *Good Times* an accurate reflection of '70s society?

Sexual revolution

Movie rating system

Do you think the sexual revolution went to far based on the current moral standards regarding sex on TV, in songs, in movies and in real life?

Billy Graham

Televangelism

Born Again Christianity

Pg. 972 **30 – CONSERVATIVE AMERICA IN THE ASCENT** King/queen of pop_____

It's morning in America. "Wait, don't hit snooze! Nooooooooooo!"

If the New Left of the 1960s promoted a counterculture, what were the bases of the platform of the New Right of the 1980s?

| Pic 973: Which do you think is the most creative sign here?

Pic 974: Barry Goldwater

a. won the presidency and influenced the rise of Reagan

b. lost the election but opened the way for Reagan

| What made Reagan turn away from liberalism to embrace conservatism?

Conscience of a Conservative

Rockefeller Republicans

Sketch out a 'three-legged stool' at right and label the legs holding up the conservative movement:

Name five important conservative publications which appeared between the 1960s and 1980s

National Review

Pic 976: Losing or at least leaving Vietnam, legalization of abortion and pornography, urban riots, forced busing and other social ills contributed to the success of Falwell's message. Why do you think that is?

| What kinds of things undermined Carter's presidency in the late-1970s?

SALT II

1980 Olympics

Did American foreign policy favor the Shah or the Ayatollah? Why?

American Voices 978. Answer the Questions for Analysis below:

1)

2)

3)

| Pic 980: What became of these hostages shown here? | Map 981: Why do you think the Indy candidate got so many votes in 1980? |

Reagan coalition

Moral Majority

Reagan Democrats

Reaganomics

Supply-side economics

Pic 982: Russian President Putin famously made commercials of him doing astounding feats like discovering treasure at the bottom of the Mediterranean Sea, or hunting powerful Siberian tigers. Are pictures like this, where Reagan is doing manly things with a chainsaw, also useful for politicians as tools to promote an image?

ERTA

National debt

Deregulation

Graph 984: When you flip through stations and land on the news, and they start talking about balancing the federal budget, you probably turn the channel. But do you think the government should be forced to spend less or the same amount that the country produces in monetary surplus in any given year?

Pic 985: How did the Rehnquist court decide on the controversial issues of the day?

HIV/AIDS

Pic 986: Youtube: *Ali G C. Everett Koop* if you want to see the former surgeon general explain why you shouldn't keep a cell phone inside your body. After that, think about the role of government in helping people deal with disease. What do these protesters want? | Pic 987: Reagan is shown here making the yard nice with tax cuts, but is this cartoonist supporting those cuts?

Lee Iacocca

Ivan Boesky

Donald Trump

America Compared 988. Answer the Questions for Analysis below:

1)

2)

Computer Revolution

Note the contributions of the following computer companies and their designers:

IBM   *Apple*   *Microsoft*

Thinking Like a Historian 990. Answer the 'Analyzing the Evidence' section:

1)

2)

3)

Mikhail Gorbachev

'Star Wars'

START

How did the Reagan administration intervene in the following places:

Guatemala   *Nicaragua*   *El Salvador*

Sandinistas

Contras

Pic 993: What was Oliver North's role in the Iran-Contra Affair?

Perestroika

Glastnost

John Paul II

Boris Yeltsin

Map 994: How did the U.S. interact with the following:

Panama   *Haiti*   *Cuba*

Pic 995: Youtube *Reagan Soviet Jokes* to see a lighthearted version of how the two leaders shown got along with each other.	Pic 996: What does the term 'psychic liberation' mean in the caption of this picture?

'Family values'

George H.W. Bush

'New world order'

Persian Gulf War

Pg. 1002 31 – CONFRONTING GLOBAL AND NATONAL DILEMMAS Hip hopper_____

At the end of history lies the undiscovered country. In this case, the America of the present and the future. Our America.

Note the final destinations of the four hijacked planes during the Sept. 11 attacks:

#1   #2   #3   #4

Relate the substance behind the two major dilemmas in American life since the Cold War:

    Globalization   *Domestic politics and economy*

Globalization

WTO

Pic 1004: If a large meeting of global power players was going on in your city, would you most likely:

         a. ignore it   b. support it   c. protest it

Why?

Graph 1005: When this charts says median family income 'stagnated' for twenty years, what does that mean?

Thinking Like a Historian 1007. Answer the 'Analyzing the Evidence' section:

1)

2)

3)

America Compared 1008. Answer the Questions for Analysis below:

1)

2)

G8

Map 1009: The core foundation countries of the European Union do not include:

a. France   b. Belgium   c. Sweden

This side of Europe joined the EU after 2000:

a. Western   b. Scandinavia   c. Eastern

NAFTA

Multinational corporations

'McWorld'

Pic 1010: The issue with subcontractors is that the company, Nike in this case, doesn't have as much oversight into working conditions, meaning they have a degree of plausible deniability as to not knowing when a scandal breaks out. What is the main demographic of workers here, and would you fit into that category of people if you lived in China?

Note three of the major 'blips' in the economies of the world thanks in-part to financial deregulation, as managed by a collusion of large banks, political lobbies and international organizations:

| Pic 1011: What does this picture say about the future of print media?

1)   2)   3)

ARPANET

World Wide Web

Patrick Buchanan

'Culture War'

Graph 1013: Today, immigration rates to America are

a. about the same as always   b. lower than usual   c. at an all time high

Pic 1012: Do you think allowing high levels of mass immigration to the U.S. while simultaneously outsourcing jobs away from the U.S. to lower wage labor markets is economically sustainable? Why or why not?

Hart-Cellar Act

What was so different about the Hart-Cellar Act than with previous immigration legislation?

Map 1014: The following four states have the highest percentages of Hispanic residents:

1)

2)

3)

4)

The group projected to rapidly decline as a percentage of the U.S. population by 2050 is

a. African Americans   b. Hispanic/Latino

c. Asian Americans   d. White Americans

This state has, by far, the highest number of Asian Americans:

What did John Hay mean when he said the following:

The Mediterranean is the ocean of the past

The Atlantic is the ocean of the present

The Pacific is the ocean of the future

What did Pat Buchanan warn Americans about in 1992?

California Prop. 187

Multiculturalism

California Prop. 209

Do you agree with the Supreme Court's decision in 2003 to allow racial preferences in university admissions?

Do you think 'diversity,' the amount of people with different ethnic or religious backgrounds, should be regulated by government? Why or why not?

American Voices 1016. Answer the Questions for Analysis below:

1)

2)

3)

| Pic 1018: Do you think Americans should be guided or driven to speak a common language? | Do you agree with the New Right that when the government began sending public assistance to people, families were more likely to break? |

California Prop. 227

| Pic 1019: Note what the following positions believe: | There have been over 50,000,000 abortions performed in America since *Roe v. Wade*. What do you think the law should be about it? |

Pro-life:

Pro-choice:

Operation Rescue

Defense of Marriage Act

How have the following decisions affected the status of the 'Culture War'?

Webster v. Reproductive Health Services   *Planned Parenthood v. Casey*

Lawrence v. Texas   *Windsor v. United States*

Bill Clinton

Al Gore

Map 1021: What do you think is the most surprising thing about the stats behind the 1992 election- and what does it say about the electoral college system?

The biggest victory of the Clinton years lay within the realm of:

    a. health care   *b. fiscal policy*   *c. foreign policy*

'Contract with America'

Newt Gingrich

Personal Responsibility Act

Pic 1022: Hillary Rodham Clinton, who would go on to run against Barack Obama in 2008 and against Donald Trump in 2016, was perhaps the most politically active first lady in history. What is she doing in this picture?	Pic 1023: After reading, what do you think? Is it fair to say Clinton 'was impeached,' or not?

Lewinsky Scandal

In 1999, President Clinton directed NATO forces to bomb Belgrade, capital of Serbia (Yugoslavia). Why did he order this attack on a European country that didn't pose a military threat to the U.S.?

Pic 1024: Note the background of the increased Islamic fundamentalist attacks on U.S. targets such as the 1993 WTC attack, the U.S. embassy attacks in Africa, and the USS Cole attack:

Al Qaeda

Osama bin Laden

When bin Laden called for a 'jihad' against 'Jews and Crusaders,' what did that mean he was encouraging?

Pentagon

Pic 1025: Describe just how 'close' the presidential election of 2000 was, and extra points if you figure out and use the term 'hanging chad':

George W. Bush

Dick Cheney

'Bush tax cuts'

Graph 1026: Look at the last column, 'Tax Rate'. Do you agree with the idea that wealthier Americans should be taxed at a higher rate, because it 'hurts them' less, or would you favor all Americans, rich, middle class or poor, paying the same flat tax rate? What do you think the best system of taxation would be?

Graph 1027: Would you say Democrats, Republicans or both have been responsible for raising the federal debt up to the record levels it is at the present time? Google: *US Debt Clock* to see what it is right now:

Sept. 11 attacks

Pic 1027: Note the death tolls during the Sept. 11 attacks:

Patriot Act

'Axis of Evil'

Bush Doctrine

Abu Ghraib

'Bailout'

Barack Obama

Tea Party

Affordable Care Act

Addenda:

Other Materials and

About this Series

Crash Course* U.S. History Guide

\# _____ *It's Review Time!* Name _____

Topic of today's episode _____

As the video goes on, summarize a few of the rapid fire points that were *not* covered in the book that seem important:

What topic or theme did "Thought Bubble" portray in this episode?

| Why did Mr. Green get shocked (or not) when he read the mystery document? | What was the correct answer? |

How did that item tie in to the material in the chapter?

Was there a 'deep' lesson at the very end? What was it?

---

*The producers of Crash Course were not involved in the production of this review worksheet.

Test Correction Guide

Time to get it right!

Corrector_____

Test Name_____

Directions: Identify the numbers of the answers you got wrong on the test and write them:

Number   Page in Book   Correct answer (written in the form of a statement using stem of question)

I got most of these wrong because…

History Movie Review

Reviewer _____

What chapter in the book is this movie most appropriate for? _____

The topic(s) it cover(s): _____

Identify some of the key characters in the movie / documentary that embody concepts in the chapter. Describe how the historical issue(s) affect the storyline in the early part of the film.

_____

_____

_____

_____

What was the "low point" or crisis for the main character(s) in the movie? How did the historical issue cause or influence that low point / crisis to occur?

_____

_____

By the end of the movie, it is probable that whatever crises or effects the historical issue was causing was resolved in some way. Explain how this turn of events came about:

_____

_____

_____

Rate this movie from 0-3: _____
3: it was intellectually stimulating and entertaining
2: it had good points but was rather dull
1: it seemed misleading or irrelevant
0: it was not worth seeing- waste of time

One image or scene that stuck out was:

_____

_____

Why did you rate it the way you did?

_____

_____

Would you recommend this movie to friends or relatives outside of history class?

_____

_____

Favorite U.S. History Textbooks

In the 19th century when U.S. history began to be taught in schools in a systematic way, George Bancroft had written the standard work, *History of the United States,* on the Colonial Era and the Revolution up to that time. Edward Channing later wrote a standard work, also called *History of the United States,* going through the Civil War. What follows is a list of the top 10 textbooks since, aside from the Henretta/Hinderaker/Edwards/Self text we are familiar with.

1. Bailey, Thomas A. et al. *The American Pageant.* 1957 and subsequent eds.
    Another very good U.S. history textbook, also still used

2. Brinkley, Alan, *American History.* 1961 and subsequent editions.
    Key text used as a standard work in colleges for many years

3. Boorstin, Daniel. *The Americans (3 vol.).* 1958.
    A Pulitzer-prize winning history of the country

4. Maurois, Andre. *The Miracle of America.* 1944.
    First came Lafayette, then Tocqueville, and then Maurois

5. Muzzey, David Seville. *A History of Our Country.* 1936.
    Taught more students American history than perhaps any other book

6. Van Loon, Hendrik. *America.* 1927.
    Van Loon won the very first Newbery medal, and does all his own art

7. Beard, Charles A. *The Rise of American Civilization (2 vol.).* 1927.
    Bailey called this book "challenging" and it is, classic college text

8. Markham, Edwin. *The Real America in Romance (9 vol.).* 1909.
    Storybook history. Worth it.

9. Fiske, John. *The New World (3 vol.).* 1902.
    One of the big historians, published after his death in History of All Nations by Lea Brothers. Problem with this it is very hard to find. Good luck.

10. Lossing, Benson, *Lossing's New History of the United States (2 vol.).* 1889.
    Classic 19th century American history read in schools and out.

Also, as an addendum to an addendum, we'll add a 'left' and 'right' history.

Left	Right
Zinn, Howard	Paul Johnson
A People's History of the United States	*A History of the American People*
1980	1999

Thank You!

If this resource book has no use for you, it has no value. We strive to make materials you can actually *use.* No waste, no filler, only usable resources with minimal marginalia aligned with the course for convenience. This is how *Tamm's Textbook Tools* works:

Coursepak A, the *Assignments* series, one you already have, has daily assignments for Monday and Tuesday (or two other days of the week, however you work it). It has the vocab, people and chapter work covered.

Coursepak B, The *Bundle* series, soon available on *Amazon* and elsewhere, has material that can be used other days during the week. This time the focus is reading comp., online activities, multimedia, video clip response forms, short answers, primary sources and free response questions (FRQs).

Coursepak C, The *Crossover* series, is the part of the *Tamm's Textbook Tools* line that stretches across the disciplines. If you teach Social Studies and want to do get an integrated curriculum crossover going with the English department, or Math, Science, Liberal Arts, or other area of the school, you would look for the particular *Crossover* workbooks that fit best. All *Crossovers* weave in material from a variety of subjects in the way your subject relates to them.

Look for these and more in the *Tamm's Textbook Tools* series, a low-cost, timesaving way to find high quality, custom materials tailor made to textbooks in many different subjects. Contact the marketing department anytime with suggestions, corrections and any other correspondence at hudsonfla@gmail.com. Find *TTT* on Facebook as well. Please inform your colleagues of the existence of this series if you think it will benefit them. Thank you.

© 2016 David Tamm

Made in the USA
Las Vegas, NV
25 August 2022